CONSCIOUS LEADERSHIP

Beyond Perception and Belief

ROD A. MACPHERSON

BALBOA.
PRESS

A DIVISION OF HAY HOUSE

Balboa Press books may be ordered through booksellers or by contacting:

Balboa Press
A Division of Hay House
1663 Liberty Drive
Bloomington, IN 47403
www.balboapress.com.au
1 (877) 407-4847

Print information available on the last page.

ISBN: 978-1-4525-3022-2 (sc)
ISBN: 978-1-4525-3023-9 (e)

Balboa Press rev. date: 09/18/2015

CONTENTS

DEDICATION

David Ronald John Stevens

I have met many amazing people during my time on planet earth. My parents Ken and Joyce Macpherson have been wonderful supporters and my children, Cara and Arlen, have inspired me while others, like John Lennon, who I have never even met, has impacted my life profoundly.

During this process of writing about the power of personal responsibility, and finding the courage to face your fears by daring to make a difference, I have had the honour of witnessing these concepts in action by way of the deeds of my friend and colleague David Stevens. Unfortunately David passed away before the completion of my book but his deeds and passion will have a lasting impact on, both me and, the wider community.

David was a member of a not for profit Board that I chair. From the moment we met, I was amazed by his energy and drive to challenge the system and break through red tape. He would always seem to find a way. David, and his partner Jamaica Magic, raised three children including eight-year-old Deisha who has suffered from a rare genetic disorder, Rubinstein Taybi Syndrome, since birth. As parents they have watched Deisha experience convulsion after convulsion as a result of her condition. They had tried every known medical option to control Deisha's seizures without success. David told me that he had tried everything and the outlook for his beautiful daughter was grim.

A few years ago the family commenced medicating Deisha with medicinal cannabis oil and the impact was immediate. The seizures ceased almost overnight. She went from having continuous attacks each day to one single event in a twelve-month period. Cannabis of any type is illegal in Australia, which made the family's activity against the law, despite the success of the treatment. That situation prompted David to take up the fight against corporate pharmaceuticals and recalcitrant politicians. He urged for legalising medicinal cannabis so that other families in similar situations could access this life saving treatment, without the fear of prosecution.

That fight is still happening. However the Premier of New South Wales, Mike Baird, has publicly spoken out in favour of David's proposal and even made a private visit to David's bedside before his death. David, being the cheeky sod that he was, took the opportunity to capture a 'selfie' of the Premier on his hospital bed and post it on his Facebook page. Only David would have the cheek to do that.

I had a chat with David a few weeks before he passed and expressed my amazement at what he had achieved. He really did not think it was a big deal but I insisted that getting the Premier to champion this change in Parliament, and follow up with a private visit to him in hospital and consenting to a bedside selfie, indicated to me that he had made some sort of impression. He agreed to allow me to use this story as a dedication in my book.

Unfortunately while David Stevens will not get to read this, the energy he channelled in raising awareness of the benefits of medicinal cannabis goes on and will gain momentum. He asked questions. He challenged old beliefs. He created change. David was just one conscious human being.

It only takes one conscious human being to create change.

Introduction

I have a theory! I have developed this theory from my life experiences as a child, teenager, adult, father, husband, lover, friend, business executive, coach, human resources specialist and general human here on earth. I find it extremely useful in managing my own life and keeping me grounded. My theory is based around the belief that;

All humans manifest as life on planet Earth, in human form, for the purpose of experiencing and learning together through those experiences. The purpose of life is to experience, learn and grow consciousness.

Let me repeat that. *All humans manifest as life on planet Earth, in human form, for the purpose of experiencing and learning together through those experiences. The purpose of life is to experience, learn and grow consciousness.*

My theory follows that once a human has learned all there is to learn, and experienced all there is to experience, they transcend this life into a much higher plane of existence.

In that elevated plane of existence, that I will call "the anything but plain, plane", they become invisible to the naked eye and hidden to other human beings of earthly origin. They have reached, what I would describe as, 'super guru' status and have no further purpose for being on this earth. They have graduated from the university of planet earth with honours. They know it all; absolutely everything there is to know. Got it all, done it all.

Like all theories this one is open to challenge. I have met many who believe they have 'been there done that' and have all of the answers only to learn later that they did not. I have myself experienced periods in my life where I felt comfortably wise, only to return to reality with a thud when I realised that I was not all that wise at all. Life is a wonderful teacher like that. Just when you think you have it down pat a new set of experiences comes your way to remind you that you still have more opportunity for growth. Not to be deterred, I have developed a daily ritual wherein I validate my status by checking the mirror. Can I still be seen? As at the time of writing this book, I can confirm that I still experience the sight of my, ever so slightly bemused, image reflected back at me from the mirror.

Bugger, it looks like I have more to learn today!

This theory has been exceptionally beneficial to me in a number of ways. Firstly, no one has been able to disprove it. I guess if someone did achieve 'super guru' status they may not be able to communicate to me in any case, as I would not be able to see them. I like that in a theory. More importantly, it keeps my ego from getting too far ahead of me and reminds me that I am here to learn and, that while I may be teaching others, I am still a student. My theory also reinforces the concept that learning is done 'together' with others and that I am not on this journey alone. Finally, it puts all so called gurus that I meet, read, view on television or hear on radio, into perspective. I can still see them! Therefore, in line with my theory, they have more to learn. That includes every single highly opinionated expert on this planet!

The fact that I can still see others, and that I myself continue to create a reflection of light that is viewable to others, keeps me grounded and gives me the assurance to write this book. I am no worse and no better than anyone else. My views and my opinions are as valid as the opinions of anyone else. My learning is unique, as is the learning of everybody else. Like all humans I perceive my environment in a different way to all others and my perception, while different, is as valid as any other perception. Therefore, I have nothing to fear and nothing to lose and, just like everyone else, I have a lot to give.

It is really only in the past twenty years of my life that I have become aware of a greater purpose to life. My first forty years were certainly a lot of fun but clearly the ego was running the show, yet I always felt that something was missing. I now know what that something was. I did not believe I was all that important in the grand scheme of things and I felt I did not really matter all that much in the big picture. I did not understand that I could make a difference. I felt powerless. I now understand that I do matter, and so do you.

Nelson Mandela beautifully captured this theme in his inaugural speech in 1994, in reference to text originally penned by respected author Marianne Williamson in her book Return to Love, which reads in part: "Our deepest fear is not that we are inadequate. Our deepest fear is that we are powerful beyond measure. It is our light, not our darkness, that frightens us". I have adopted this profound thought as a running theme of this book to help illustrate how, as humans, we have come to think that it is safer to sit back and choose to believe we do not make a difference, rather than understand that we all can and do make a difference, and take responsibility for it.

While my theory may serve to remind me of my real value in life it equally reminds me that we are all students on this planet. We are all still learning. We are none of us complete and all of our unique set of experiences and learning are just as relevant as those experiences of anyone else.

During this book I will express a number of beliefs and theories that underpin these views. I do not profess to have the answers. I certainly have plenty of questions. What I do propose is that the views and opinions expressed in this book are no less valuable and relevant than any other views and opinions expressed in any other book or media outlet. Life is a unique experience. These are my unique views formulated from the experiences and observations from my almost sixty years on this planet.

So what prompted me to write now?

For many years I have become increasingly frustrated with the behaviours of humanity, and me sometimes as well. I can't help but think there is a better way, an easier way. I struggle with the continual bombardment I experience, through a basically hysterical media, of less than loving behaviours regularly demonstrated by our leaders, both politically and in business. We just have to be better. The world is clearly struggling on a number of levels.

Our world is struggling to survive when our destiny is to thrive.

I was born and raised in the beautiful Australian state of Tasmania. Tasmania is often ridiculed for being caught in a bit of a time warp but to me that is one of it's most endearing features. There are people in Tasmania that have never travelled from the island state and who never will. Why would they? Tassie is clean, green and safe. Well in relation to many other parts of the globe anyway. When I was growing up it was indeed a beautiful and safe place to live.

The current situation on our planet reminds me of a classroom experiment at Kings Meadows High School in Launceston, Tasmania. The year was 1969 and my biology teacher was a wonderful British gentleman that I knew as Mr Perks. I was not the most attentive student at school, but I was always fascinated with life and, in particular, the workings of the human body. Mr Perks was a charismatic gentleman with a knack of making his classroom fun by using experiential methods of learning. That means he was practical and preferred his class doing stuff rather than just reading. I must admit that while I really engaged with pretty much all of the practical learning I never really took to the dissection of frogs! I distinctly recall one particular class when Mr Perks conducted an experiment in a small petri dish containing cotton wool soaked in a sugar food liquid (don't start me on sugar). We added a microscopic bacterial culture to the dish and observed it over the coming weeks.

The bacteria began to multiply and grow as it consumed the food source. It was quite spectacular in colour and complexity under the microscope. What started out as a small barely visible microscopic dot on the edge of the dish exploded into life. The bacteria had no predators within the dish and continued to populate spectacularly. The environment in the dish was perfect for this extraordinary life form. Within a matter of weeks this amazing bacterial colony dominated the dish until it completely covered the entire surface of the cotton wool. At its peak, the bacterial community was a colourful and intricate organism and a perfect example of vibrant life.

However, as time went by we watched the entire culture lose colour and, just as quickly as it exploded into life, we witnessed it quickly die. It had consumed all of the food resources in the dish and could no longer sustain itself. Sound familiar? This is where I believe humanity is headed right now unless we change.

Even as a fourteen year old school trouble maker, I recall thinking - 'Wow this is just like people. We really need to respect our environment'. As it turns out we have not done particularly well in heeding Mr Perks' simple lesson. Like that bacterial culture, humans continue to consume and exploit our environment in search of enduring economic growth, which in a finite ecosystem like earth, is clearly unsustainable. I struggle to find leaders in business or politics that really appreciate this concept. It seems to me that individuals that hold this view either do not go into politics or boardrooms, or are excluded and branded extremist environmentalists, or just plain nut cases. I am certain that there are role models out there somewhere but how do we, as a community, connect and support them in light of our highly censored media.

I have some personal experience from the Franklin River dam protests that dominated Australian and Tasmanian politics during the 1980's. For those unfamiliar with this notorious event, the Franklin River is an amazingly pristine fresh water source that flows from the Central Highlands of Tasmania through some incredibly beautiful and untouched wilderness, steep rain forested gullies and gorges, en route to joining the Gordon River before eventually emptying into Macquarie Harbour on the wild west coast. At the time, the government of Tasmania had approved the construction of a hydroelectric dam on the river, which sparked a national protest, and ultimately lead to the formation of the Australian Green Political movement and the rise to prominence of Dr Bob Brown. Federal Government intervention, and a subsequent high court ruling on 1st July 1983, eventually stopped the dam. While this represented an enormous victory for the environment, to be living in Tasmania and to be a conservationist, was quite an intimidating experience.

I was working for a major bank at the time and many clients were pro development supporters. It seems that jobs and money were more important than the environment. Nothing has really changed all that much has it? I was certainly shunned for my personal views and felt compelled to keep them to myself, as best I could, for fear of possible repercussions from peers, and my employer. I became a cupboard conservationist. One Saturday evening a passionate pro-development football mate of mine hurled my favourite 45rpm single "Let the Franklin Flow' from my living room balcony into my back yard. If my memory serves me the party ended shortly after that. I did eventually retrieve the treasured vinyl from my garden in the morning and it remains one of my favourite tunes. Even now that song still evokes a strong passion for my native Tasmania and our beautiful earth. Fast-forward thirty years and it is apparent that those that stand against progress that threatens our environment still face derision and intimidation from the powerfully wealthy pro-development faction.

I read of, and speak with, people that express the very same frustration that I feel but nothing seems to change. I watch our politicians and business leaders display the very same unconscious behaviours displayed by the single cell bacterial organisms in Mr Perks' petri dish and feel powerless to stop the madness. It seems that there is general consensus that the world is out of balance and at the very same time a belief that we are powerless to change it.

I often reflect upon the lesson that I took away from that high school experiment. I am a practical person and I look for the cause of a problem rather than treating symptoms. In the case of our planet the symptoms are greed, sickness, fear, over population and separation. This leads to a society with a burgeoning population growth that a few rich families and powerful corporations profit from through uncontrolled exploitation of our beautiful life-sustaining environment and it's inhabitants. That is what we see.

The cause of this madness, however, is our seemingly complete lack of consciousness. That is what this book is about. How do we raise our level of consciousness? That is how I propose we restore our earth and save ourselves in the process. It is up to us. It has to be us.

For if not us then who? By being passive observers we are actually giving permission for the insanity to continue. We are actually a part of the problem. What if we are "powerful beyond measure"? What if it is only our fear that is holding us back? It takes courage to recognise your own power.

I do not wish to continue to be part of the problem. I want to make a difference. I want to face the fear of my own light. I believe that the world can change but we need a revolution. Not another war but a revolution in the way we think and act. A revolution on an individual basis: one by one. A revolution by evolution. We are at a tipping point in the history of our existence. We need a totally new slant on leadership and the responsibilities we all have to our fragile planet. We need leadership that understands the concept of higher consciousness and accepts that our earth is just one big organism and that nothing happens in isolation. We need leaders that accept the existence of a greater intelligence that created and maintains life. We need leaders that are compassionate, able to operate from the heart, yet able to accept there are natural consequences from actions and that natural process must be respected.

If we are to survive as a race, and a species, and an economy, **quality conscious leadership** is critical and the solution is shared responsibility.

There is no invincible hero in a red cape on a white horse, wearing his underpants on the outside of his trousers, riding in with shied held high to save us. The problem is of our making and likewise the solution. We must grow up as a race and face our fears. We must face our greatest fear, the fear of our own power to make change.

Chapter 1

The Time is Here Now

I can hear the question now, the very same question that I have asked myself over many decades. What can I possibly do to change the dysfunction in this world? This is far bigger than me. What difference could I possibly make? I am only one person. I believe the answer to these questions lies in the expansion of human consciousness. I believe that we are at the dawn of an awakening, an evolution in human consciousness. It simply has to be. The time is here right now.

Let me clarify. In this evolution of human consciousness, our history and the lessons from our past will be, and are, a part of our conscious evolution. Those experiences occurred as a part of our journey. Our greatest lessons come at times of our greatest pain. I think we have all experienced that horrible moment when we get caught doing something we should not be doing, dreaded the consequences only to find later that we learned one of our biggest lessons from the experience. Or perhaps it was some tragedy in our lives that changed us at a deep level. Some of the horrific experiences that we see daily are happening to get our attention. We can no longer hide. The more seemingly painful the experience, the greater the lesson and the greater the opportunity for growth.

The pain that our planet and our people are currently experiencing presents a perfect platform for change.

But who is going to lead the change and how do we learn our lessons? I for one was becoming extremely impatient about the arrival of our saviour, whoever or whatever that saviour may be.

While writing this book Australia experienced the tragic death of a young test cricketer Phillip Hughes. Hughes was just short of his twenty-sixth birthday when he was struck by a cricket ball on the back of the neck, just below the lip of his protective helmet, and died on the playing surface at the iconic Sydney Cricket Ground during a first class cricket match in November 2014.

Phil Hughes was a talented country lad who had a dream to represent his country. He left his small hometown of Macksville in northern New South Wales, a short journey south by car from where I am writing this book, and ventured to the big city of Sydney to pursue his dream. He represented his country at both limited overs and test level, all in his early twenties, before falling from favour and struggling with his game and his confidence.

I never met Phillip Hughes. I worked in Macksville for a period as the HR Executive for a company that employed his older brother Jason. I imagine that Phillip had the very same passionate approach to life that I observed in the then nineteen-year-old Jason when we were discussing his intention to follow his younger brother to Sydney to pursue his own sporting interests.

The tragic passing of Phillip Hughes on November 27, 2014 had a profound affect on me personally and on the wider Australian community. His funeral was televised live on all channels, something I could not recall happening since the 9/11 tragedy. I pondered how it was possible that his death could have such an impact on so many people regardless of whether they followed cricket, or any sport for that matter. Was it the loss of such a young man in his prime of life? Sadly that happens all too often. Was it the untold story and potential this young man still had to give on the big stage? But then many talented young stars have passed before without such fanfare.

The closest events with such personal impact on me were the death of Nelson Mandela, the tragic passing of Princess Dianna Spencer, the Princess of Wales in 1997 and the senseless murder of founding Beatle John Lennon in 1980. What is it with these particular individuals that evoked such empathy and connection and how does the tragic death of Phillip Hughes even remotely compare with these other iconic legends? Each has special talents in his or her own right, but what is it exactly that was resonating with me? The traits that sprang to mind were vulnerability, transparency and authenticity – the ability to acknowledge personal fear and failings but do it anyway, regardless of what others may think.

My own life has been substantially impacted by the life of former Beatle, John Lennon. My very first record, a 45-rpm single, was the double sided 'Day Tripper' and 'We Can Work it out' from 1966. I saved my pocket money for weeks to get that record. Through the evolution of the Beatles, and Lennon's personal battle with drugs and the meaning of his life, I followed his ongoing confrontation with the establishment in the pursuit for world peace, his subsequent withdrawal from the music industry limelight and his amazing rebirth as an artist and human being, abruptly ended by his senseless shooting in 1980. We all witnessed publicly his failings and his sensitivities. He was always authentic. He put himself up for ridicule. The media taunted him and he let go of any attachment to his popularity and image as a Beatle to express his personal pain and beliefs on world peace. Imagine! We all thought he was mad. Looking back now he seemed to be one of the only sane humans on the planet. Ultimately Lennon was just a man. I recall a videoed conversation of him with an avid fan and autograph hunter. Lennon was puzzled by why the fan wanted his signature. What was so important about a signature? He said something along the lines of 'the significance is in the music and the words of the song not in me'. He made some profound statements and wrote insightful lyrics that continue to hold relevance for us all.

The life of Princess Dianna had a similar theme, authentic and sensitive. Not perfect by any means but real and caring beyond her self. Born and married into royalty we saw her imperfections in public and she took the ultimate risk and opened her heart to us all. We saw the human side of the royals. They are just imperfect people like the rest of us! I believe witnessing the flawed side of Princess Dianna created an avenue for connection with the rest of us. We all know our own vulnerabilities and can relate to that in one another. Dianna Spencer showed us that she was just a woman after all.

Mandela carried the same remarkable character qualities. A life typified by hope and passion mixed with those special imperfections that gave him a sense of reality. Nelson Mandela was no saint. Nelson Mandela was passionate and authentic. It is easy to forget that he was a young activist before he went to prison. Mandela was very human. I believe Phillip Joel Hughes was of that ilk. Passionate and driven yet not possessing the perfect cricket technique. He worked on his game and on himself with vision of greater ambitions, and yet a humility and vulnerability that was there for all to see.

But wait, Lennon was an iconic rock star. He sold more records that anyone previously and the Beatles, well they are the Beatles for goodness sake! Dianna Spencer, she was a British royal. British royalty dominates mainstream press across the globe and Mandela well that was a story for the ages. How could his heart wrenching fight for equality from a prison cell and the resultant progression of South Africa into racial freedom not captivate the planet? Phillip Hughes was just an Australian cricketer and not even in the current test side! Why was I, and so many Australians, captivated at that moment? I couldn't help but feel that there was more to this than just the loss of a talented and likeable young man.

It came to me as I was reflecting on this book early one morning. It is the time. The time is here right now. People are ready and wanting to heal. Humanity is looking for authentic, honest and conscious humans who have the courage to pursue their dreams with honesty and integrity in spite of their fears. We value them. On a deeper level we all want to be like that. I believe that we have a yearning to own our light side and face our own fears. We possess a deep ache to have the courage to face our personal inadequacies and stand up despite the possibility of rejection and ridicule. We are becoming tired of following like sheep.

There is a growing sense of frustration manifesting on planet earth in regard to the way we are destroying our fragile environment, and ourselves, in the pursuit of financial growth, despite the multitude of warnings and evidence that things have to change. We seem powerless to stop this. We witness politicians and business leaders promoting their own agendas in childish and dangerous games while irresponsible mainstream media pushes the boundaries of truth to sell advertising and satisfy their owners' corporate greed. We are continuously confronted by senseless conflicts, atrocities and destruction in the name of religions that all inherently promote peace and kindness.

And all the time we look for a leader to step up and make sense. Barack Obama is one who I believe speaks openly and has a vision greater than his own political ambitions but we have witnessed him hamstrung by a political system that has evolved to ensure that the real power is seemingly not with the people but with a small number of grossly wealthy and powerful corporate moguls. There are others like Obama across the globe no doubt that wither in the system and never even get the opportunity to rise to prominence.

In Australia our current political options are totally devoid of leadership quality and authenticity. No wonder voters are disillusioned with our democratic system! We seem to have created a mixture of corporate sloth and popularity chasers.

My feeling is that people have had enough. The Internet has served to bring us information direct from the source without the censorship of the mainstream media. We have more alternate information than ever before. We are at a tipping point. We know things have to change but we do not know how. What can we possibly do? And then along comes a plucky country kid that captures our imagination. A kid high on integrity and low on pretence, prepared to be the subject of ridicule but never lose sight of his dream. We connect to those sorts of real heroes. We want real people. We want truth. A part of me recognises that the Phillip Joel Hughes phenomenon was not so much about cricket or sport but more about people seeking truth, something real yet vulnerable. Something genuine. After an explosive start to his test career when he was being compared to the greatest test cricketer of all time, Sir Donald Bradman, Hughes had been banished from the side and floundered at state level. But he was a fighter. He had a dream and he persevered. He was on the cusp of a recall to the test side when he was tragically taken. He had never given up on his dream. That is what I have taken from his passing.

This book had originally been about more traditional leadership models and the changes that current and future leaders would have to possess to lead us out of our current spiral. I have certainly been yearning for heroes who are true to their very core, that are not perfect and possess a sense of vulnerability just like the rest of us. Role models that consistently strive to do better and are brutally honest with us, and themselves, and who hold the beacon that we will follow.

I understand now that waiting is simply not an option.

It seems that we have all been waiting around for that next Jesus or Mohammad or Buddha to make it all right for us and save humanity when the truth is, it has always been up to us. It is up to each and every one of us to play our part in our everyday lives at being authentic, conscious and vulnerable. None of us is perfect. That is evidenced in my theory. Just check your mirror if you have any doubt. John Lennon still had a reflection and certainly Phillip Hughes still had a reflection.

But guess what? It is just fine to have a reflection. It is perfectly ok. What is not so ok is to turn away from what is happening on the planet and wait for someone else to ride in and save the day while we allow our lives to be compromised by our lack of consciousness. Nelson Mandela could not ignore the inequality. John Lennon could not ignore the madness of war and the ludicrous idolisation of pop gods, and Dianna Spencer could not ignore the greater part that she had to play as part of the responsibility that went with her station, despite her own human frailties. Each made sacrifices in the pursuit of their ideals. Why would anyone want to follow that path? Surely it is easier to sit back and be a wallflower? That is a much safer path - or is it?

While we are prepared to take a back seat in the interests of our own safety, our planet and humanity, including us along with it, is slowly dying. Our inaction is actually destroying us all. We are the new leaders. We are here now and we alone have the power to change things. It is not up to our children or someone else. It may well be too late if we delay and leave it to future generations. All of us, together, must take responsibility and we must take it now. Humanity is facing extinction. The time is upon us.

As Lennon alluded to in the classic Beatles rock composition 'Revolution', it's not about hate and it is certainly not about violence. It is about mind set. It is about attitude - "We all want to change your head". It is about taking personal responsibility and being true to your real values while accepting your shortcomings. It's about getting up when you are knocked down. It's about going back to basics when you fall from your path and slip into complacency. It's about consciously doing what you can in your own life to become a better leader, a better human being, a better person, a better father, a better mother, a better son or daughter or bank teller or doctor or cricketer. It's about having the courage to speak out when you see something that is clearly wrong, or does not feel right to you. It's about growing up as a race and saying 'enough is enough'. There is another way.

That is what Phillip Hughes and John Lennon and Princess Dianna and Nelson Mandela brought to the table. That is what I connected with. You don't have to be famous - you just have to be conscious and follow a purpose. You just have to be real, have a dream and be brave enough to pursue it. We can all do that.

———

In the following chapters I will touch on some of the universal truths that have been around for millennia and that aspiring leaders in a highly conscious world will need to know. These truths apply regardless of whether you believe in them or not. Some you may know and some may challenge you. All I ask is that you keep an open mind. Only you can decide what is true for you.

The most important thing we all need to know, and particularly if we are in any position that may have an influence on others, is who we really are ourselves. That is our own self-awareness. What makes us tick and how do these so called universal truths impact our lives? This is a key to leadership into a conscious world. Without self-awareness we get more of the same.

We can, each and every one of us, make a small difference every day and that is all that is needed to make a big difference and create change in our world. The slogan "think globally and act locally" is very relevant. Individually and together we hold the key. I liken this power of small actions making a big difference to the theory of the one hundredth monkey. Lyall Watson and Lawrence Blair published this theory in the mid 1970's in a publication called Rhythms of Vision. The theory originates from stories of observations documented by unidentified Japanese scientists, studying the behaviour of the Macaque Monkeys, on the Japanese Island of Koshima in 1952. While this theory may have some factual inconsistencies the theme is very appropriate to human learning and consciousness.

Apparently the monkeys being observed on Koshima were all eating sweet potatoes that were consistently covered in sand from contact with the island beaches. Despite the gritty taste, the monkeys still consumed the potatoes, sand and all. It follows that one-day a single monkey started to remove the grit from their food by washing the potato in the water before eating it. This behaviour was gradually taken up until a critical number of monkeys, supposedly one hundred, were washing at which time all of the other monkeys converted to the new behaviour in quick succession.

Furthermore, it is claimed that the behaviour then spread to a neighbouring island at around that same time leading to assumptions that the new found consciousness of the monkeys had somehow spread there. While some of the facts in this story have been disputed over time, the theory is still sound in that behaviour is mostly learned from what is happening in our environment and there is a point when that behaviour becomes the norm. As more people start to change their behaviour, and live more consciously, then others will learn from their actions and at some point that behaviour becomes the accepted practice. There is a tipping point. There is power in numbers and the numbers are you and I.

I don't know about you but I am well and truly over the sand on my sweet potato and I know that I am not the only one. One by one we can make a difference and change the world. All you really have to do to change the world is change your own perception of the world and your own behaviour. It is that simple, just your own.

We are all leaders. We all have the ability to influence others and create change.

Chapter 2

SELF-AWARENESS – WHO ARE YOU?

If there is one thing each and every of us simply must get to know it is ourselves. This is the single most important piece of knowledge you can learn in your lifetime and also the only piece of knowledge that you, the individual, can ever uniquely know. Who are you? What makes you tick? Why do you feel the way you do? Who are you and what are you here for? What is your purpose?

Awareness is a determining factor in being conscious. The difference between the animal kingdom and humans is that we have the ability to experience ourselves. You will learn as you progress through this book, and from your own experiences, how the ability to experience yourself can be a double-edged sword.

Later chapters will cover other important information, also referred to as 'universal truths', which impact all of us. However, our own knowledge, understanding and acceptance of our own selves are critical in a functioning human being seeking to raise their own consciousness. Understanding ourselves and raising our consciousness will ultimately raise the consciousness on our planet. Conscious leaders understand themselves and accept they will experience life differently to others.

Every single human being on this planet is unique in some way yet exactly the same in others. We all have a unique interpretation of life, and what we see as reality, yet at a spiritual level we are all connected and of the same source. Our life experience is different yet our death experience is the same. I will leave the death experience for a later chapter but suffice to say that once we transition from this human life, and lose all attachment to our bodies and our egos, we are all united in the same eternal universal energy field. However, while living a human experience the only way you can even begin to understand what an individual person really thinks and believes is to actually be that person. And even then it is not as easy as it sounds. It is simply not possible to completely understand who another is because we never fully understand who we are ourselves. We may share feelings and beliefs with trusted and intimate friends or lovers and, as a trusted friend; we may even feel that we do fully understand what another is all about.

There are no two people exactly alike and our perception of life will always be unique. We all experience a different perception of life.

Let me explain. Before we are even born there are energetic factors that will impact our later perception of life. Energies from our biological parents before conception will impact on the energies comprised in the ova and sperm that join at conception. All of our cells contain energetic memory. The nine months of the experiences of the maternal mother are passed on to the unborn child through her energetics. In addition, the planetary influences at the time of birth create variances in universal energy flows that all contribute to our uniqueness before we even take our first breath. We enter our world as literal learning sponges, an almost blank canvas if you like, but not entirely.

It is well documented that the first five to seven years of our lives are the period where we integrate most of our beliefs and patterns into our subconscious mind that later play out in our adult lives. The child is a bit like that blank canvas. The child has no ability to differentiate information it receives from family, friends, teachers and the external environment. A child takes this information in as truth. It has not yet developed any filters. Unlike a fish, that has the intelligence to swim and feed from day one, a human baby is totally dependent upon its parents and it's environment to support it. The developing child learns from that environment so that it can survive. Children will adapt accordingly.

A child does not filter information during its formative years. If told over and over that it 'never does anything right', it will take that to memory. That memory will, later in life, manifest as a core belief at a deeply subconscious level. Those combined memories intrinsically impact the filter that generally develops in children from around seven years of age. I like to think of this individual filter, that we all have, as a pair of unique tinted goggles we wear which give us an exclusive colour and tone to our environment. Once our filter is in place we then subconsciously process all incoming information through it. At a level below consciousness, we decide what is true and what we each choose to ignore. It is important to note that not all of the information we choose to ignore is inappropriate; it is only our distinctive filter that decides that. To put that simply, before we have developed our filter we accept everything we experience as truth. Once we have a filter in place then all experience and information is subconsciously filtered before we accept it as truth.

It is near impossible for any of us to really know the factors that may be at play in our own daily lives because of the variety of influences that have impacted our filters, let alone for someone else to understand them. We all have different lenses in those goggles!

It is important to understand and accept that filters exist in all of us and that these filters are all unique. That is why we all perceive reality differently and that is perfectly ok.

Let's go back to the beginning. The most important thing that we need to know is ourselves. I should clarify that a bit further. Because of the filter creating process, I have just described, it is practically impossible to 'know' all of those factors that made us who we are. A more accurate terminology than 'to know' is *to accept*. Accept that you have a unique filter just as everyone else has. Accept that you may never know all of the influences and patterns and beliefs that reside deep in your subconscious mind and equally accept that they surely do reside there. Accept that we all see things differently.

This will give you some comfort in a world of conflict and competition. We all see the world differently. Even when you think that you totally agree with another there will surely be discreet differences. You just won't necessarily notice them. Take the colours that we see for instance. What if the colour that you know as red was actually green to me? That is I saw the colour green instead of the red that you see. You would say red like a cricket ball and I would say yes that's right but actually I would be relating to a green coloured ball that I have come to know as your red. You would never know that this difference existed, and could never know. It is impossible to communicate that difference because we both have a unique perception of the colour red and, because we allocate that different colour to the same objects, we will always think that we are seeing the very same thing when in fact we are not! Life is like that.

So how do you know yourself if you don't know what went into your own filter? Great question! If you can accept the filter explanation as true then you can start to work on getting to know how your filter impacts your perception on reality. The important things to accept are:

- You have your own unique filter
- Everyone else has their own unique filter that is different to yours
- All information, and therefore our reaction to it, is influenced by these filters
- At a spiritual level we are all connected

Feedback is a wonderful way to find out more about our filters and ourselves. I will go into more detail around the pitfalls in giving and receiving feedback, and the affect of core beliefs on that process, in chapter six. However, processing input from those around us is an important aspect of learning about us. You could say that our whole life experience is pretty much about collecting feedback from those around us, and our environment. I will focus on personal feedback for now. It helps if we think of our entire world as a mirror.

What we perceive is entirely a reflection of what we believe.

We project into the mirror and we receive information back that we use to support what we believe. This is particularly relevant in close relationships. Our close relationships provide the opportunity to see deep inside ourselves and we do not always like what we see. Close personal relationships provide one of the most challenging, and at the same time rewarding, experiences for human beings. We get the experience of the mirror up close and personal. Relationships are 'in your face' and, more often than not, give us immediate response to what we have projected as to who we think we are. Naturally, we do not always agree with the response. It is then convenient to blame our partner for our ills when what they are in fact doing is reflecting back what we are broadcasting. To change the reflection you see in a mirror you need to change the light reflecting onto it. Always remember that our perception of our reflection in the mirror is coloured by our beliefs and filters and that it is far from the truth of who we are spiritually.

Intimate relationships are a fantastic way of letting us observe and fully experience the world of our own ego.

Our lives are basically experienced in two states. Predominantly we are in our ego state. This is the standard human experience of fear, time and space. In this state our egos are in play, literally. This is what I refer to as our life situation. The other state is our spiritual state. Death is one way of experiencing this state permanently but not necessarily recommended as a way to enhance your personal consciousness on earth. Alternatively, we have windows into this spiritual state when we shut down our minds and are totally present and conscious in the present moment. Meditation is an effective way of connecting with your true spiritual being in a place where ego does not exist. Fear cannot exist in this higher state. Fear is solely an experience of the ego state.

The highly conscious leader understands that there is more to life than the human experience. A highly conscious individual understands that the ego represents the human life experience and that in truth we are much more.

If we take it as given that we wish to continue to participate in the 'human life experience' then our egos, and the accompanying filters that cultivate fear, will be in play. Human egos are influenced by fear. Fear can manifest as guilt, greed, hopelessness, anger, control, jealousy or any other feeling that cannot be aligned with joy and love. Our natural state of spirit is the joy being. Joy is that feeling you get when you are in awe of a magnificent sunrise or watching a tiny kitten playing and you are totally present in that experience.

The current level of world consciousness results in fear dominated decision-making. Whether it is the need to be massively wealthy, to control large corporations, to adopt a radical religion or to work in a job that we are not passionate about, just to pay the rent, fear is the driver. The media sells fear. The stock market sells fear. Governments sell fear. Parents sell fear. Schools sell fear. Corporations sell fear. To an extent we all buy it.

Armed with this knowledge we have a choice to be materially successful in our human experience by selling fear, just like nearly everyone else, or we can look at alternate ways to be materially *and spiritually* successful without fear. After all, the universe is abundant and continually expanding. There is no lack.

It is certainly not a bad thing to have wealth. It is certainly not a bad thing to make a profit. Only we can assess whether we are manipulating a situation, and in the fear business, or if we are acting from compassion and love and an understanding of the higher truth of who we really are. Only one of those choices will heal the earth. The fear business is a terminal business. It is not sustainable. Any leadership or management guru will tell you that fear is purely a short term motivator. We can see what fear has done for us over the past few millennia! Empowerment is the way to truly engage people. Empowerment is allowing people to exercise their own light and make conscious choices. To be empowered we have to be informed. To be informed we need transparency.

Lets take a look at a topical situation in politics. Australia has experienced a lengthy economic boom mainly spurned by the expansion of resources through the mining sector. Previous governments have spent without an eye to the future. The boom has been on the way out for some time. The reality was always that adjustments to spending would have to coincide with reductions to revenue streams, or alternate revenue streams would be required. The result of these changes has seen the country going from a healthy surplus to a burgeoning deficit approaching a trillion dollars.

From a family perspective, that simply means going from having a big savings account to having a massive overdraft.

A real leader in government, driven from compassion and operating from the heart, would be open and honest about the situation. Popularity is not important. The truth is important. A highly conscious Prime Minister would ensure that his team was focussed on the challenge and then seek long term solutions from as wide a scope of sources as possible to come up with a balanced plan of action that addressed the real issues. A highly conscious opposition would appreciate the challenge facing our country and seek to impact policy with constructive suggestions, without political point scoring.

What we see in the Australian Parliament is a government that is more focussed on a next term in power and an opposition that would do anything to make sure that does not happen. The Prime Minster is fearful of losing his position and Leader of the Opposition will take any opportunity to promote fear to have that happen. This is a perfect example of the fear business. It matters not which party is in power. This is an example of unproductive, short-term thinking, lacking integrity and based around fearful considerations. Rather than transparency we are offered mistruths and misconceptions meant to confuse us all. Our governments fear empowered voters because informed and empowered voters will see right through the charade. I sense that is happening already.

Unfortunately, this type of behaviour is prevalent in business as well. I observe fearful people, afraid of losing their power or money, selling fear to maintain their own security. But guess what? It does not secure their safety and it does not stand up to scrutiny against the laws of nature and of the universe. These mind antics are simply playing in the space of the ego. This behaviour does not transcend fear, nor does it contribute in any meaningful way to the elevation of consciousness on our planet. These behaviours represent individuals deep in the fear business operating from a level of ego. They are not yet able to, or not yet choosing to, accept that their perception on reality is unique and no more relevant than anyone else's. They are not accepting that everything is connected at a spiritual level and, that by taking advantage of or hurting another, they are in effect hurting themselves. They are not accepting that their fearful thoughts only create more fear. They are clearly caught up in the game of life and forgotten that it is only a game and not the truth.

Put simply, a human being can be described as being of two distinct parts. The first part is the thinking part, or ego, that feels disconnected from others, that worries, is competitive, judges what is right and wrong, is educated, rich, poor, good looking, fat, charming or ugly. The other part is the spiritual part, often referred to as the soul, which is connected to everything that is.

More than ever we need leaders that can access that other part of who they are and champion the truth, not popularity, and know when their own egos are active and how to make decisions that are not adversely impacted by their own filters, which as we have already established, they do not fully understand themselves in any case. We need each other. Our beliefs and filters prejudice our own perception of reality. Only by operating from beyond that filtered perception can we know what is real. We need to understand that what we see as red is not in effect red to everyone else.

Knowing and accepting this reality, it is possible for all and any of us to make our choices from a higher level of self-awareness. It is possible for us to lead conscious lives that contribute to the healing of our planet.

Yes, we can study at the most expensive university on earth and accumulate a fistful of degrees, certificates and letters after our names, enough to fill a standard business card to the brim, yet the most valuable piece of information that we can ever learn will always be who we really are and our acceptance of the power of our own light. Without that understanding we are just another pawn in the fear game.

Well the game is getting ugly and it is time for a new way.

Chapter 3

WE ARE ALL ONE – THE QUANTUM FACTOR

Before any of us are able to take the lead of our own lives, or lead teams or organisations, there are a number of universal truths that we need to know. Universal truth is distinctly different to your own beliefs. Universal truths affect everyone, regardless what they believe, while beliefs only affect the believers. Universal truths are theories that have stood the test of time. Of course the truth is only valid until it is disproved and we are still learning. Universal truths support the underlying principles of many spiritual beliefs and quantum theories. I should remind you all that I still cast a reflection and therefore stand to be corrected at any moment! Here is my slant on how this all fits together.

Our beliefs form part of our personal filters. Beliefs are very individual, although there are groups, such as religions, that share similar broad beliefs. While we all have the choice to believe something or not, something that is a universal truth will still apply in our life regardless of whether we choose to believe it or not. Beliefs, on the other hand, can be changed and once changed no longer apply in our lives. A universal truth will apply regardless. It is wise to understand the difference.

For example the work of a trapeze artist is subject to the law of gravity. To ignore gravity would be at their peril and make their activity, not only extremely dangerous, but also quite impossible. The act of trapeze does not work without gravity. It does not matter whether the artist believes in gravity or not, gravity is in play.

The single most important truth that humans must know and accept is that *everything in the entire universe is connected.* This may well be the only truth we have to know. Many other universal laws apply because of this one element.

Quantum physics, also referred to as the new science, is teaching us that everything on our planet is, at the most micro level, connected vibrating energy. That's right, everything! And so it follows that the earth is not separate from the rest of the universe and everything living and existing on earth is connected to earth. We live in a relational universe. Everything relates to everything else.

Every thing that exists is connected and no thing is not.

Separation does not exist in quantum reality. However, humans generally see themselves as separate due to the way our physical bodies and minds experience our world. The human brain only detects a minute amount of information from the plethora of available data. Even then, that information is impacted by our own life experiences and beliefs that make up our unique filters. In effect, the minute portion of information that each of us is able to interpret is done so on an individual basis. We all interpret life differently and that gives us the experience of separation from everything else. That clearly explains why we are not all Collingwood supporters!

You can liken the human brain to a receiver of information and only able to tune into a small portion of the total signal. This is not too different to a television or a radio. There are countless channels being broadcast on the airwaves but, like a television or radio, our receiver can only be tuned to one signal at a time. So each of us is listening to, and watching, a slightly different channel and thinking all the time that this is the only channel on the air. Unlike a television, humans are also broadcasters. This particular human skill will be covered in more detail in chapter five when considering our creative abilities and thoughts.

This one quantum truth of connectivity accounts for a number of other laws of the universe including the Law of Attraction. The Law of Attraction is the basis by which we create. This law works at an energetic vibrational level. Thoughts are made up of vibrating energy. Yes, thoughts actually exist. When we put out certain thoughts into the universe they align and attract other similar frequency vibrations. Our thoughts are our own unique broadcast signal. This principle works similar to a tuning fork which, when tuned to a certain musical frequency, will resonate with like tuned sources. This law is an essential consideration for leaders in a highly conscious world. We need to understand that everything that we see and experience is exactly what we have attracted and we have a choice to change those experiences. We have our very own remote! Our remote is called choice.

What a shambles! Everything is connected and yet we all see and feel things uniquely. We are all connected and yet we mostly feel separate from each other? We all have access to the same information and yet we all receive and interpret it differently? Our thoughts are constantly creating and attracting and yet we seldom know when and what we are thinking. This goes a long way in explaining the current situation with humanity.

That part of us experiencing separation, and consequently the fear that goes with that experience, is referred to as the ego. The ego is who we think we are. That of course is not who we truly are. The ego is the sum of all of the factors that influenced the subconscious mind of the child before, during and after birth. I prefer to view the ego as the part of us that reflects who we think we are (personality) as opposed to our spiritual being which is who we really are (universal energy). The ego has several aspects. One aspect is often referred to as the inner child. Some refer to the inner child as a separate entity and many healing modalities are very successful in treating emotional health conditions by dealing directly with an inner child entity. For simplicity I prefer to see the inner child as an aspect of the ego. That being the case, the ego then is also the part of us that has a lot of fun and play. The ego is not all bad. It reflects our personality in our material existence. The ego can be light and playful. Have a look at our politicians' egos playing in question time in Canberra. Play school for egos. If it weren't costing us all so much it would be damn good entertainment!

The ego is not evil although it can be. The ego is controlled by fear.

This dilemma of the human ego is perfectly illustrated in religion. All religious origins have a common theme, although most have been radically distorted over the centuries due to man's own fear and subsequent need to control. Fear and control, rather than love and compassion, drive religions and much of the behaviour, associated with religions, is fear based. Whether that be terrorist actions of radical religions, we are witnessing in Syria and Iraq, or the more understated use of heaven and hell in more mainstream groups. Regardless, the common thread is fear. Do what you are told and you will get a cushy place in heaven sipping Pina Coladas, otherwise you will roast in hell with a daily whipping from your worst enemies.

If you trace the origins of most religions, the common theme alluded to the existence of a greater loving intelligence, or God, that created and protects all life. I have absolutely no attachment to any religion but I do have strong belief in the existence of a greater loving intelligence. I call that entity universal energy, or God is ok with me as well. This higher intelligence, in the deepest sense, is often referred to as pure unconditional love.

The new science has established that everything is made up of the same vibrating sub atomic particles, or vortexes of spinning energy. We are all made up of that same energetic stuff. I often call that energy God stuff, although giving it a tag like that is not all that useful. You can only know of God stuff and not actually see it. One thing for sure, God is certainly not an old codger with a grey beard sitting on a big comfy chair sorting out who is good and who is bad, like I was told when I was growing up. It is important not to get caught up in having any attachments to name tags. Words can be clumsy and I apologise in advance for any confusion that you may experience through the use of my nametags for different things. That is my official disclaimer by the way. The important thing to remember is that at the most micro level everything is connected by the same intelligent stuff.

Humans have an ego that is who we think we are. The ego thinks it is separate from everything else. However, we are all made up of the same connected vibrating energy.

Everything is connected. There is no separation. This is a popular conception of both spiritualists and quantum science and essential in our understanding the way forward in the quest to save the planet. The connecting force is the energy of God stuff, or pure unconditional love, or whatever you want to call it. As I said the name is unimportant.

Man, in his unending search for answers, is actually finding more evidence that supports the existence of this God stuff. Why on earth we need to prove the existence of what created us I have no idea. You only have to look at the beauty and complexity of life to know that life is a not random creation. There has to be a higher wisdom at work here. I should clarify when I say 'man' I use that term to include both sexes, although I must admit as a man that the male gender has a lot more to answer for in regard to using fear in manipulative religions, sensationalist media and ruthless business than our female counterparts. I plead guilty as charged!

I recently watched a documentary out of war torn Syria. In this documentary was a child of no more than four or five years old. The child was surrounded by the rubble of shelled buildings and masked militia holding guns. The interviewer asked the boy if he was afraid of what was happening and he said "No I am only afraid of God". How have we allowed that to happen? How can an innocent child believe that the very loving energy that created all life could possibly be feared? Conscious parents, aware of who they truly are, would surely never allow that to happen.

Man has built the enormous Hadron Collider, expressly to smash the smallest imaginable subatomic particles, in a futile attempt to find the source of life. But he will not find this mysterious God stuff because, like everything else in the universe, man is made of it. We do not have to look anywhere outside. We are all actually made of pure unconditional loving energy that many refer to as God. John Lennon once referred to God as "a concept by which we can measure our pain". I like the poetry but leave the interpretation to you.

I have already explained that our human experience, and particularly that driven by thought, will only ever be capable of detecting a tiny portion of the massive pool of information that exists around us. Our brains are only capable of receiving a tiny fragment of the reams of data and messages flowing freely through us in every nano second of our lives. Even the data we are able to receive is then deciphered by way of our own filters and prejudices. Albert Einstein surmised that the observer influences every experiment simply by the intent of their observation. He was alluding to the fact that creative forces of thought have an impact on observation. That is another consequence of total connectedness.

It is basically impossible for humans that are seeking answers and outcomes to detach from the outcomes they seek.

In summary, we all see and experience life differently. These differences are a direct result of a number of things including, but not limited to, the time of our birth, the experience of our biological parents, hereditary factors and the external environment during our childhood and beyond. It is not as important to understand what factors made us develop our current beliefs as it is to understand that we do have these subconscious belief systems. These beliefs are not often evident to us, and can be reprogrammed through our own consciousness. These individual belief systems are what give us the experience of separation from everything else and make up our ego. This is who we think we are and not who we really are. This belief in separation gives rise to conflict, greed and fear. We think we are alone. We believe that we are in competition with everything else and must struggle to stay on top. We forget that we are in fact a connected part of everything and, as a part of everything, it is cooperation and not competition, we must embrace.

It is estimated that ninety five per cent of our thought and responses, and subsequently actions, come from our subconscious mind. When we are not in a state of high awareness, and operating from our conscious mind, we are defaulting to a subconscious response. That subconscious response manifests as our ego state.

Our ego is similar in nature to a part we are playing in a Broadway production. Just like the actors in the play we take a part and act it out and just like the actors in the play we can choose to take another part and act that out if we wish. It is important to understand that our life situation is like a game and not reality at all. When your parents told you that your part in the play was as a support, and not a lead part, you accepted that as the truth. The truth is that we are vibrating energy with the ability to create and manifest whatever we want. Anyone can be whatever he or she wants. Any of us can take the lead part at any time provided we can overcome 'our greatest fear'.

I likened humans to receptors and broadcasters of information, tuned into a different channel and picking up a different set of frequencies. Our thoughts represent outward transmissions and inward messages are felt as feelings. We tend to think of the universe as a massive material machine when in fact it is more of a huge pool of thought. Think about that for a moment. We all have the ability to adjust our frequency and receive other channels just by adjusting our beliefs. We all own the same kind of radio but we all have our reception set to a slightly different station. Some like heavy metal and some like classical. The thing is we don't always understand that we can change the dial. I can assure you that you can change stations. You do have choice.

I am personally fascinated by the science of Quantum Physics. For those wanting a more detailed explanation there are a number of wonderful books in circulation that will give a more profound insight into the factors impacting our human experience than I ever could. Bruce Lipton has an intriguing book "The Biology of Belief" which has some wonderful details on the relationships between energy and biology while any modern psychology text will also outline some of the intricacies of the human mind.

Quantum science is forging a path that is increasingly aligned with many ancient spiritual beliefs. The science is providing an energetic explanation for various ancient spiritual philosophies. This represents new learning that simply must be taken into account with existing theories and beliefs. These new findings cannot be ignored. We must be prepared to modify or discard out dated philosophies. Just as there was doubt and resistance when humanity moved from the flat earth theory to one of a circular globe, there will be a degree of discomfort as we accept our energetic connections. There was still fear that ships could drop off the horizon, despite clear evidence to the contrary. This is what we are experiencing right now. We have more information now than at any other time in our history and it is our fear that creates the resistance to change.

Despite our different views on life and the world around us we are all made of the same stuff. We are all connected. We are all a tiny working piece of a greater organism, made up of even more minute particles. We are all vibrating particles of light energy. More importantly our minds are all tuned in to a different set of stimuli even though we all have the same channels available to us.

We are all God stuff vibrating in perfect harmony as a part of the intricate soup of life. This is something that we should always remember and celebrate often.

Chapter 4

THE MYTH OF HUMAN SEPARATION

Human life is precious. Human life is a connected part of all life and therefore all life is precious. Life is precious. It follows that human life can never be more precious than life itself! This is simply not possible as human life is a part of all life.

The single biggest factor in the destruction of life on planet earth is the flawed belief that humans are separate and have more right to life than anything else.

I understand that these views may be challenging to some. There is, however, substantial scientific evidence that all life, as we know it, is connected and therefore of equal value. Separation only exists in our minds (ego). Rather than knowing ourselves as intricate parts of all life, we experience ourselves as competitors with other life forms on our planet. Additionally, in this material world of ego, we are subject to the laws of nature. Our bodies can be injured, die or even be eaten. Materially we are a part of the animal kingdom called nature.

In the ego state the laws of nature impact humans. We are of the animal kingdom. The primary law of nature is that life is cyclical. Life on earth arises from seed, or fertilised egg, and eventually dies as part of a pattern known as the cycle of birth and death. In nature, a seed is fertilised, grows and matures and at the end of the life cycle (death) the eternal, vibrating energy, which makes up the living organism, returns to the soil to nurture more life. Like the breath in and out of our bodies, and the destruction and formation of far away stars, the universe is in constant cycles of birth and death and nothing is ever lost. Yes folks God is recyclable. Humans tend to view death as an end of the life cycle. By nature, a cycle has no end and no beginning. A cycle is endless.

Death is merely a transition of energy from one life cycle to another. Nothing is ever lost. We are all fully recyclable.

If we look at the components that make up all known matter in our world there are a limited amount of known elements and, according to quantum discoveries, at the base level all matter is just vibrating energy. From what we know these components cannot be destroyed. A property of energy is that it cannot be destroyed, only transformed.

As already stated, I have absolutely no affiliation to any religion. I have faith and I have beliefs but I do not subscribe to any religious doctrine. Therefore when I refer to death as a 'transition' I am not talking about reincarnation, although the concept of our energetic consciousness existing in every living thing does fit broadly with that particular religious belief, along with some others. What I am referring to is the vibrating consciousness, the vibrating energy, of a human life never being destroyed by physical death, but rather the energy of that life recycles back into the universal energy field as part of a greater living organism. It is important that all of us, and in particular leaders in decision-making positions, understand this concept.

In truth, there are no life and death decisions or situations.

Human life is not separate from the intelligent life force from which it is created. Just as a fish in the ocean is never separate from the ocean, and is unable to survive without the ocean, human life is always a part of the universal pond of life and could not exist without it. Herein lies a major problem with mankind; the belief in separation and the belief that human life is different and more important than other life forms. This idea results in the bizarre behaviour that we see all around us wherein humans seemingly have little consideration for other life forms or our living environment. The great majority of scientists now believe that this selfish destruction of our planet for profit will end with the extinction of the human race. This destructive behaviour, demonstrated constantly in our political and corporate world and replicated in many of our own actions and thinking, is clearly 'unsustainable' and based around unfounded fear. Current human behaviour can only be described as total and utter madness. Yes you heard it here first, we are all totally bonkers!

If we look at the human body at a micro level it is made up of trillions of individual living cells working together in harmony to sustain a human life. At a sub cellular level each cell is either made up of, or actively interacting with, much smaller vibrating particles that I will refer to collectively as energy. This is what science currently understands is the base structure of all matter. Energy is described as 'a property of objects that can be transferred to other objects or converted into different forms but cannot be created or destroyed'. At the most micro level then, all human matter could easily be referred to as vibrating particles of energy and each of those subatomic particles of matter is a part of life. In fact they are the building blocks of all life, although I expect that there is still so much more that we do not yet know on this subject. The point is, the more we explore the more we realise that all matter is connected and made up from the same vibrating energy. The difference between a rock and a human, it seems, is the level of consciousness. It could therefore be concluded that, as rocks have done far less damage to our planet than humans, rocks actually contain a higher degree of consciousness that we do? Yes rocks, rock! Well on the surface anyway. Please do not share this finding with any rocks just yet.

In the life cycle of a human being, cells are created and cells die. The death of a cell does not damage the larger organism in fact it is just part of the growth process. I remind you that we all originally started out as two individual cells at conception and that death is no more than the end of the cycle of our physical awareness of life. The vibrating energy that makes up our being will never be lost. It can't be lost as energy can only transform. Death is like a full stop after a sentence and not the end of the book, or for those familiar with vinyl records, it is the end of the track and not the end of the album.

Death, as we experience it as a part of nature, is perfectly normal. Death is not the end it is simply a part of a natural cycle of life in a material world, and a transformation to another cycle of life.

The same principles can be applied to any business and the global economy. The human economy is subject to the very same rules. It simply has to be because everything is connected and nothing is separate. There will be death as part of any cycle of life. That is a natural part of a healthy system. However, just as most humans do not want to die and will seemingly do anything to hold on to life, regardless of the implications for life itself, business has the very same fears and does not want to die either. This fearful thinking by corporations, industries and government institutions is another reason why we have driven our race, and our planet, to the brink of destruction. Our behaviour is driven by fear arising from the belief in separation. We believe we must fend for ourselves or else be destroyed. We are driven by fear manifesting as greed and the need to control our environment.

Giant corporations dealing in oil, coal, pharmaceuticals and medicine are enormously powerful and will not relinquish their position quietly. This is despite burgeoning evidence that these industries are in fact destroying the very living environments that support them and they are, in effect, killing themselves as well. They are resisting their natural cyclical death, or transition, and in doing so taking the rest of us along with them.

The cells in our own bodies are continually dying and being replaced with new cells. It is estimated that during any seven year period that all of the cells in our bodies would be 'new' cells. Just imagine if every cell in our bodies had this insane fear of death as demonstrated by multinationals?

Envisage a situation where every cell ever created wanted to live forever and would do absolutely everything to continue to grow and expand, regardless of the health and ongoing viability of the larger body. Imagine if each cell simply continued to cling to life within the living organism. Can you conceive what a mess the body would be with all of those continually multiplying cells? In essence that is what we call cancer! Cancer is the abnormal and unnatural growth of cells that seemingly are not complying with the natural life cycle of healthy cells. Yes a healthy cell has a life cycle and that is what defines it as being healthy! The behaviour of cancerous cells could be compared with what we see happening to our earth. In this case it is humans and corporations that represent the cancerous cells clinging on to an unhealthy life.

Death is merely a transition. Life cannot be destroyed. The energetic particles of consciousness that make up life will always be in existence.

Accepting this truth does not mean that we no longer value human life or the endeavour to save life. Compassion to save another life is a beautiful part of who we are. It is a wonderful part of life and a quality that elevates us above other animals. However, that compassion for life must extend beyond humans and we must equally accept death as a natural part of life, and not something to be avoided at all costs. Remember we are all connected. Despite us being able to experience separation we are in fact a part of a much larger living organism, our earth.

To only value the human aspect of life is like a person exclusively protecting their right hand and allowing an infection in their left toe to go untreated. The end result of that narrow view, on a functioning human body, would be the eventual death of the whole body. And so it is with earth, economies, industries, countries and communities. We must accept the notion of the whole organism; we have to accept that everything is connected. If we do not we will certainly get more of what we are getting and I for one would like to see that change.

Let us focus on industry for a moment. Can you see any comparisons in the behaviour of industries to unhealthy 'cells' that left untreated would transition (die) into a renewed form? Lets look more closely at the coal industry as an example? We all know that the burning of fossil fuels is not only unsustainable, as we are dealing with a finite resource, but damaging and destroying our living environment. Just like the infected left toe it is pouring poison into our system that will eventually kill the larger organism. Yet governments, mining companies, power corporations and trade unions will fight tooth and nail to protect an industry that, in reality, should have died naturally long ago; but why? Our own Prime Minster only recently said publicly that coal was 'good for humanity', which is a bit like your doctor saying that smoking was good for your lungs or that war is just healthy competition. Despite the fact that many people are employed in the coal industry and related activities, the industry is poisoning us and should be allowed to pass away naturally. There is absolutely no healthy purpose to be served in maintaining coal on life support.

So why do governments, business and unions resist the natural cycle by clinging to dying industries? They each do it out of fear. The government justifies its resistance as protecting the economy and to appease controlling stakeholders, and of course to retain their own hold on power. The owners protect shareholder profits (generally they are substantial shareholders themselves) and their often-obscene salaries and personal power, and the unions protect workers jobs and their own power base. Unfortunately, we let it happen because it is all too hard or we simply believe what is told to us by the aforesaid stakeholders, through mainstream media that directly benefits financially from the coal industry interests in some way or another. Holding onto a terminal industry because of fear of lack is as crazy as holding on to your breath for fear that there might not be another breath to follow. Both actions have the same outcome. Unconsciousness. We must have faith. There are alternatives.

The harsh reality is that none of the leaders in this group show any appreciation of the bigger reality, or they simply choose to ignore it. None seems to understand that everything is connected, or accept the bigger picture, and none in any way accepts death as a part of life. These fearful behaviours are actually preventing new business life from flourishing. Just as the rotting plant returns to the earth to fertilise the new seed so to the decaying energy in the dying industry transforms into a new venture. Nothing will be lost when you take a higher view. Such attempts to support a dying industry are futile in the face of natural forces and have glaring consequences for us all. If you have any doubt about the consequences, go and stand near a coal fired power station for a few hours and witness the junk spewing into our beautiful clean air or fly over an active coal mine and view the damage done to our land.

I would suggest that the owners of obsolete industry, such as coal, transition their investment into alternate, sustainable forms of energy. There is one hell of a power source that shines above us every day. If we had invested the same amount of capital into the development of harnessing the energy of the sun as we have on the extraction of coal we would have all the power that industry and consumers could ever use, without poisoning our environment. To crudely use a phrase from Monty Python's Life of Brian we would have "all the power we could eat". The only reason that the capital has not been invested in solar is that companies cannot own the rights to the sun. Similarly, with the pharmaceutical and medical industries can you imagine the impact on the billion dollar profits if people knew that they could heal themselves by changing their thoughts? Business cannot own your thoughts with a patent, like they can medicine, drugs, treatments or even worse, genetic modification. I will expand more on this later.

It seems that anything that is free has no value to corporate giants yet we know that the best things in life, such as health and love, cannot be bought.

I would ask governments to stand up for our global environment and implement innovative policies that incentivise alternate industries and create employment in sustainable, cleaner energy sources. Government policy is an extremely effective way to influence the market. Phase out tax incentives for polluting energy industries like coal and offer incentives to develop solar and the market will respond. The problem is that corporate billionaires influence (control) our government and would never support that sort of policy. Hey don't we elect our government? Did I mention that democracy is flawed? I will talk more on that later as well. Governments already use tariffs and subsidies to support, what would otherwise be, unsustainable industries, including oil and coal. How about using these measures to develop truly sustainable practices instead of keeping dying industry on life support! Of course when any such sensible action is touted the fear machine, that is corporate media, on behalf of vested interests and through manipulated politicians, will publish enough fearful commentary to scare the pants off us all. Mostly lies of course but then fear is never concerned with truth is it?

If you ever want to get close to the truth of any matter then it is wise to follow the money trail. When facts and stories are promoted it is always wise to know who benefits the most and who do they control. This is information that we need to know to make informed choices. We saw obvious conflicts of interest during the demise of the tobacco industry. There was any number of specialists wheeled out by tobacco giants that categorically denied smoking cigarettes was dangerous and that smoking did not cause cancer. We now know this was all manipulated by the industry and yet we continue to hang on every word from drug companies, about their miracle medications and vaccinations, when we know that they are the direct beneficiary from the product to the tune of trillions of dollars. I prefer to listen to people that neither derive direct benefit from the product, nor responds from old subconscious fear. The challenge is who are they and where to find them?

I would urge trade unions to support their workers transition into the new jobs created by viable, sustainable industries. In doing so they not only protect jobs but life itself. If the purpose of trade unions is to protect jobs and workers rights then what does it matter in what industry the jobs exist? Unfortunately union executives, while on the other end of the political spectrum to corporates, are in the same fear and power game and seemingly are more interested in protecting their own relevance and power base, along with supporting the election of their political party, than engaging in meaningful job transition outcomes. Surely billionaire corporate types would not influence union leaders? Money corrupts both ends of politics. We are not that gullible, are we?

In any case, the whole notion of employment and jobs being the most important consideration in government decision-making is clearly ludicrous. We use that out dated and fearful thinking to justify opening new mines, in pristine environmental areas, on the pretence it will 'create thousands of new jobs'. What baloney. Are our jobs really a priority over our life-giving environment? The importance of having an income is drilled into us as kids as a reason for being here on earth, but that is old paradigm thinking. We are on earth to fulfil our true purpose and do the things we are passionate about, not out of fear of being less, or having less that someone else. There is plenty to go around. Take fear out of the equation, so we all feel safe, and replace that with love and compassion and we can all live truly fulfilling lives doing what we enjoy, in the knowledge it is right for us and our earth, without the constant struggle for material wealth.

Jobs are not the priority. Doing what we are passionate about and with purpose is.

It is critical to our own survival that we question all that we read and see in the media and have the courage to express our opinions and ask the questions that need to be asked. One question that springs to mind is why do we still mine and sell coal and what actions are in place to stop? What is being done and why is it taking so long? Corporates will respond to pressure, eventually, especially when it hits financially. Is anyone out there still investing in tobacco shares?

Business, government and workers have much to gain if they can only let go of what is dying and work together on what is growing. We all have so much to lose if leaders in these spheres continue to only focus on their immediate need to control their environment, out of the fear of having, or being less.

We all have a lot to lose if we don't support and display the leadership characteristics linked with higher consciousness, including acceptance that we are all a part of one complex living organism. No one cell has any more or less importance in the function of a healthy human body and so it is with our earth. Some humans may think they do but that is not the truth. We all live or die together regardless of our wealth, position, colour, religion, sexual preferences or political persuasion. Being wealthy does not buy you life. Life is indiscriminate like that; it wants all things to thrive. The challenge facing us all right now is to get this message out and remind the world that it is our responsibility to make the change. We are all important. We all matter.

As Ghandi famously said "be the change you wish to see in the world".

Chapter 5

Emotions and How We Create our Reality

In any aspect of our lives, whether it be family, relationship or career, it is imperative to understand the concept of creation. Our thoughts create our perception of our reality and our reality is only our perception. What you think about, you become, and what you are and experience right now, is a summary of what you have been thinking about previously.

Life is only our perception of what we think is happening.

That can be a difficult concept to grasp but let me assure you that it is an old truism and a basic assumption of new science. Everything in the universe is made up of vibrating energy. You could say the universe is vibrating energy. This universal vibrating energy is a powerful intelligence.

A thought is a form of energy. Thoughts can be measured and are made up of vibrating energy, just like everything else.

Energy seems to take the illusion of two basic forms; materialized energy and unmaterialised energy. Materialized energy is more familiar to us because that is what all material and physical things are made up of, vibrating energy. That includes you, your car, your home, your mobile phone, your desk and your staff. All are simply materialized vibrating energy. The rest of the universe, that we do not see or experience, I will label as unmaterialised energy. We don't know so much about this but that is not important at the moment. No doubt there are many other things that we do not yet understand. Everything that we do 'think' we know as materialised energy was at some time unmaterialised and was created into form by thought. The universe is pretty much a huge pool of thought. All that we see in our lives originally began as thought and was created from unmaterialised energy. Of course our thoughts are influenced by our beliefs.

With that in mind, you can see that our thoughts are immensely powerful. Do we always know what we are thinking? How do we know what we have been thinking in the past? Just look around. Who you are and what you have, and what is in your reality, is a direct result of what you have been thinking. If you are not well it means that you have been thinking unhealthy thoughts. If you are poor it means you have been thinking lack, and if you are insecure then you have been thinking fearful thoughts. The good news is that change is only a thought away. How wonderful! We can step back from our lives, look at what we have and what we are, and know that by changing our thoughts we can become something totally different if we want to. We have control.

Thought creates our perception of our circumstances and changing our thoughts will change our perception and our perception is our reality.

Of course nothing ever seems simple does it. It is estimated that the average person generates around 70,000 thoughts a day. Yes 70,000 on average! That equates to around fifty a minute or very close to one every second! People are basically super duper, walking, talking, thinking machines! How many of your thoughts do you remember? If thought is the first step in the creative process, and we constantly think, then how can we possibly change that many thoughts and be able to change our lives? The answer lies is in our emotions.

Emotions are wonderful guides. Emotions are the feelings that separate us from the rest of nature.

Emotions are a whole body experience that validates the thoughts we have created against our connection with the universe. Emotions are felt by all of the cells in our entire body and they harness a lot of energy. Everything in the universe is connected. Our emotions 'feel' our thoughts and experience them in relation to our own beliefs, exposing them to the greater universal energy field, of which we are a part. This is not a conscious process for most of us. Our emotions often just seem to come up from nowhere and we often struggle with them. The fact is that reading our emotions, and understanding their message in relation to our thinking, is something that can be learned. Many businesses have become exposed to the notion of Emotional Intelligence as a part of their leadership development. This innovative learning process basically involves honing intuition through understanding our own emotions, and the emotions of others. Intuition is your higher self simply validating your thoughts and beliefs against the universal intelligence. Let me explain that a little further.

Thoughts are created, either consciously or unconsciously, in the mind. I did not say the brain because the human mind is more than just the brain. Some unconscious thought may be initiated by cellular memory from any part of our body. I believe that deep-seated trauma, or even past experiences, are held in our brain memory as well as in various other cellular memories. An interesting thing to remember is that each of our individual fifty trillion or so cells has the very same components as each other. They may have different functions within the body but each has basically the same makeup. So brain cells have the same basic internal functions as muscle cells, and all cells have intelligence.

A thought then, whether we are aware of it or not, once created becomes a part of the manifest universe, in that it is measureable energy, and interacts with all that is. As we are a part of all that is, and not separate, we are now also connected to the created thought and can experience it. Lets say the thought was triggered under stress from an old belief that we were not good enough. Our first experience of that thought could be one of feeling inadequate or embarrassed, which is felt as an emotional response. Of course this emotional communication is tainted by our own unique beliefs, some of which are known while most are hidden below our normal level of consciousness.

For example I am entering a crowded room and begin to feel anxious. If I allow my fearful thoughts, now manifesting as an anxious emotion, to take control I would possibly turn around and leave the room. But there is no apparent danger in this room. My conscious mind knows that I am healthy and safe and have been invited to speak to a gathering of people, and many are known to me. Why the emotional reaction?

At a level below consciousness I have created thoughts that say I am not good enough and that people will judge me and I will not measure up to their expectations. This is likely a carry over from early childhood as most core beliefs are entrenched and learned before the age of seven years. Maybe my father was not good with crowds and passed that fear on to me? Maybe I had a bad incident at school where I was embarrassed in front of my peers? Some people spend lots of time and money trying to trace where their damaging beliefs came from but that to me is not really important. The main thing is to understand that you have subconscious beliefs and that you do not have to be a slave to them.

In the above situation my emotions have converted the subconscious thought into feeling and now I have awareness of the thought through my emotions. I have a cold sweat and shallow breathing. Of course I could ignore the emotion, override it and hold it inside but this is not a healthy thing to do. Emotional energy is very strong and the suppression of this energy is a form of resistance that can lead to illness in many forms. This is not dissimilar to building a dam on a flowing river. The pressure of water behind the dam will build up over time and eventually breach the wall, or collapse the whole structure, with potentially sickening consequences. Let the emotion rise and flow. Acknowledge it and feel it. Reinforce the truth that these physical emotions I am experiencing are coming from a thought that carries some fear, a thought that has no relevance to right here and now, a thought from the past with no meaning today. I know I am safe. Now consciously replace the original thought with a more accurate one from your 'desired' belief system. Your desired belief system contains the beliefs that you want to have, beliefs that support a happy, healthy and successful life. The new thoughts could be along the lines of; "I am happy with who I am. I am safe. I do not judge others or myself and I do not allow others to judge me. I am complete. I am ok with who I am."

If you have practiced this process, and developed a strong belief in your new affirmations, then the emotion will change to reflect the message from the new thought. Easy? Well if you believe it is that easy then it is that simple. I should point out that those old original beliefs have been in your cellular memory for many years, and been reinforced thousands of times, so it makes sense that some consistent and strong intent and action will be required to create permanent change. There is a school of thought that a new habit can be formed in twenty eight days if practiced consciously every day. I have the view that beliefs are similar in nature. The old belief, or pattern, will have established neural pathways in your brain that will take time to fade. This is why it is easy to resort back to old habits of thought when you are not paying attention. The old memory will never totally disappear. This is similar to a walking track through a grassy field. A well-worn path will instinctively attract new hikers because it looks used and familiar. It takes time to wear a new pathway but as more hikers tread that new path and wear in the track it will eventually become the route of first choice. By consciously changing your thoughts you are in effect establishing a new pathway and the more it is used the stronger it becomes. A bit like building a muscle really.

Do your beliefs serve you well? If not then get some that do.

There is an alternate view that emotions come first and then the thought afterwards. While that may be the common experience what is really happening is that the thought has come from your unconscious self and you were not aware of it even being generated. We would all be exhausted if we were consciously generating seventy thousand thoughts a day! The emotion from a thought may well be the first indication of the creative process set in place. We may never consciously be aware of ever generating those thoughts but that does not change the fact that we did. Just accept that you did and replace it with the thought that compliments the experiences you wish to create.

In summary our emotions and feelings are the body's way of letting us know what we have been thinking. Humanity has become very good at masking emotions. My personal belief is that this is a root cause of many psychological and physical health issues. Emotions (feelings) are critical in a functional and highly conscious human. Emotions are what makes us different from the rest of earthly life. I personally spent a big part of my early life battling with emotions and doing what I could to keep them out of sight. The occasional burst of anger was possibly the only indication that this was happening but inside I was experiencing an ongoing battle to keep a lid on what I was truly feeling. Eventually I had the breakdown that I had to have to survive.

Like many baby boomers, born in the fifties, I was told to toughen up. Big boys don't cry. Having a stable job and financial security were the priorities that I learned from my parents. I learned to make sacrifices to climb the corporate ladder. I had lead a fairly shallow, yet highly enjoyable, existence in my youth yet all of that time I had this deep feeling that something was missing in my life. In company, and in social circles, I felt complete yet when alone, or in a reflective moment, I felt empty and could not understand why, particularly as I seemed to have everything that I could possibly ever want. Well all of that came crashing down as I entered my forties. Welcome to the mid life crisis!

I was in a senior relationship position with an Australian bank. I had just returned from five years in an overseas posting and was re-evaluating my life. I had bottled up a high level of frustration from my own internal clash of values with those of corporate Australia and my confusion as to who the hell I really was. Looking back, this is what many would refer to as a mid life crisis. I was around forty years old at the time. Externally I seemed to have it all. I was outwardly healthy with two beautiful children, superficially happy marriage, fantastic oceanfront home and a well paid job. Internally, however, I was unravelling at a great rate of knots. I experienced anxiety and developed depression, which I now understand to be a result of my own negative thoughts. I became suicidal. I had it all worked out. An accident on my motorcycle would not arouse any suspicion. I had actually convinced myself that my children, Cara and Arlen, and the world for that matter, would be much better off without me. I was well insured. All debts would be cleared and my kids would benefit from a very nice legacy with which to enjoy their lives. As for me, well I would be out of this unimaginable sadness that I found myself constantly enveloped in. Even as I write this down it all sounds quite absurd to me now. But the human mind, influenced by ill conceived beliefs and manifesting from an unconscious state driven by fear, is a very dangerous thing.

My life could have gone a number of ways. Certainly suicide was my popular choice until one evening my life took an unexpected turn. I had separated from my wife and had custody of our children on a week on - week off basis. My beautiful seaside home had only sparse furnishings and an unhappy feel that mirrored my own internal situation. I had a residual debt from my divorce settlement and little belief in my future or my personal worth. I had forgotten that I had choice and that I was an important part of life. I had forgotten that I was connected to all life. I felt alone.

I arrived home late one evening, from my well-paid corporate job, which I detested, and slumped onto the dilapidated sofa I had inherited as part of my divorce settlement. I recall bursting into tears of deep sadness. My son Arlen, who was around nine years old at the time, heard me and came and sat beside me. He put his arm around my shoulders and said in the most loving manner "Don't cry dad. Everything will be alright". That simple act of compassion turned out to be a life changing moment for me and set me on the road to recovery and fuelled my quest for higher consciousness. While the story of that journey is for another book, Arlen's kind words that evening opened a window, enabling the light of awareness to shine deep into my soul. At that moment I could actually see the sad victim role that I was playing and I wanted to step up and take some responsibility for my life. I recall saying to myself internally "What are you doing? You are the parent here. It is you that should be looking after your children, and yourself, not the other way around". I saw myself right then as a pathetic slave to my depression and I did not like what I saw. I made a conscious decision then and there that I was going to get myself back on track and take responsibility for my own life. And so my journey took another turn.

The point of my story is, we must honour our feelings and appreciate that they are coming from our deepest thoughts. Feelings and emotions bring us strong messages. We must also be mindful as to the relevance of the thought that triggered the emotion. We know that the majority of our thoughts are fear based, originating from a time and place that no longer holds significance to us now. An equally important message, learned from my experience, is that a small gesture of kindness can have such a huge impact on someone else.

I conveyed this story to my son Arlen around ten years later and asked if he remembered that evening and how it saved my life and changed me profoundly. His reply was a simple "Nah". Teenagers, what can I say. I did take the opportunity to remind him of the power we all have to impact others. His simple and heart felt words truly changed my life, even if he did not know it.

We can all make a difference in others lives through small acts of random kindness. Never underestimate the power you have to enable change in another. A smile in the street, a compliment in a store, an unexpected thank you or a phone call to a friend to tell them that you love them can have enormously powerful impacts on another. It seems that we get so caught up in our busy material lives that we forget that life is only a game after all and only as real as we want to believe and perceive. We get lost and forget what is really important and that we can, and do, make a difference. Maybe it is just another symptom of our forgetting that we are indeed 'powerful beyond measure'?

The journey is not always smooth but we can change our part in the drama of life when we have the intent to do so. Things are never entirely as they seem.

Chapter 6

Choose Your Beliefs – It is Your Choice

The leaders needed to steer humanity into a world of higher consciousness must understand that we all have choice. Choice is a God given right. The leaders we need right now must understand that they have choice and accept that everyone else also has choice. There are no victims. There are only those that are not yet aware they have choice. A key responsibility of any leader is to make others aware of their right, and indeed their responsibility, to choose.

One of the most empowering things that I have learned during my own life journey is the existence of choice. Once you get that, there is no reason for anyone to be a victim anymore. The truth is that we all have unlimited power over how we experience our lives, our health and wellbeing. After all, our life experience is merely our perception of the small amount of information we manage to capture from our universe, processed thorough a filter that we barely even understand. The story I shared in the previous chapter was the experience I needed to have to realise that I had choice.

One of the critical choices we have is the choice to select our beliefs. You are not restricted to any particular belief system. You can believe what you want once you understand that you have choice.

Lets look at some common beliefs and the consequences of simply accepting them as truth and not exercising choice. Religion is an interesting one to start with.

Where do our religious beliefs come from? Usually they come to us early in life from family and our immediate community (environment). If, for instance, you were born in the Middle East in a Muslim extremist family you could quite conceivably find yourself, as a young adult, walking into a crowded market place with explosives strapped to your chest with the aim of causing as much destruction and loss of 'infidel' life as possible in the name of Allah. Both you and your family would accept this as a honourable thing to do and there would be no feeling of guilt associated with what others, living another reality, would describe as an act of terrorism. You would expect to be honoured in death. You would be considered a hero and promised great rewards in the afterlife. In this controlled environment that this child was raised, it is difficult for the individual to exercise choice. After all there were not a lot of alternate ideologies available to learn or consider. Even so, the fact remains that this individual still had choice but had no awareness of that choice. Is that really having a choice? Perhaps not.

Imagine then that this religious extremist had an identical twin that was, at birth, adopted into western society and raised as a conservative Christian. How would that twin view the act of violence by their brother? We have two genetically identical humans from the same parents, born at the same time and at the same place and yet with radically different perceptions of life. Who is right and who is wrong? The answer depends entirely upon what you believe.

The truth is that everybody is always absolutely right in his or her own reality. They have to be.

In Australia, most would find any act of terrorism unacceptable and quickly label it as an extreme act of murder and undeniably wrong. On the other hand, the extremist Muslim community would find the sexual freedom enjoyed by western women as equally appalling and wrong. So who is right and who is wrong?

In the world of the ego there is no absolute right or wrong. Your judgement of right and wrong will be formulated based on your own beliefs and chosen values. Therefore in the world of ego, everybody is always absolutely right. They have to be. After all what makes one person's beliefs more relevant than another's? We were given the right to choose after all.

The awareness of choice is the key to getting what you really want. Knowing what you really want, however, is entirely another thing!

In human reality an individual's truth is basically *that which they assess as being in line with their our own beliefs.* I have suggested that, at a level of higher consciousness, there are universal truths that apply to everything that are not subject to personal beliefs. For example everything is connected, we are all a part of an intelligent universal energy field and that our thoughts create.

The concerning aspect to the example of the suicide bomber is that they have had no choice in the beliefs they have adopted. Rather, these have been inherited, or indeed it could be said, forced upon them. This is how we develop many of our deepest subconscious beliefs. We took our childhood beliefs on without question and without exercising choice.

Have you ever experienced an argument where you know what is right but the other person just does not get it? How frustrating? What is wrong with this person? Why can't they see this simple fact? Guess what, they are thinking the very same thing about you. I saw this demonstrated recently in a Facebook conversation over vaccinations. Two extremely well educated people with opposite beliefs on the ethics and benefits of vaccinations. Both protagonists produced, supposedly indisputable, factual evidence to support their own views with neither willing, nor able, to accept any part of the others argument. The end result, after some rather insulting and crude language, was that both left the conversation even more convinced in the truth of their own belief. But who was right and what is the real truth?

Everyone is always right, in his or her own mind, and life is lot easier once you accept that fact. A conscious thing to do, when locked in disagreement, would be to listen to the other person's point of view and try to understand their beliefs. It does not mean that you have to agree but you just might learn something about this person, and more importantly, about yourself and your own prejudices. This presents an ideal time to learn more about your beliefs. Whether you like it or not, you are connected to everything, including your adversary. At an energetic level they are just another part of you.

We each have a multitude of beliefs that we have accumulated throughout our lives to date, and in particular in our formative childhood years. Some we can identify and talk about while others sit at a deep subconscious level and we may never have awareness of them. These are some of the key beliefs that drive our behaviours and, quite often, are the beliefs that we do not consciously identify with. Like our breathing and our heartbeat they operate automatically without our conscious thought. More often than not we get to exercise our hidden subconscious beliefs during times of stress or conflict. Stressful days at work, or in close relationships such as family or our partners, are ideal situations to bring up these hidden treasures. Have you ever calmed down following an argument with a close friend or partner and thought 'why did I react like that and say those things that I do not believe are true'? At some level you probably do believe some of those things are true as a result of a variety of past experiences that have, over time, assimilated into hidden subconscious beliefs.

Our actions are often driven by beliefs that we do not consciously associate with or understand.

Now that is a scary thought. It certainly would explain why people that we think we know so well do such extraordinarily strange things when under stress and why close relationships are so challenging. I have heard a number of stories about people that committed suicide despite outwardly giving the impression that they were quite happy with life. From my own personal experience, suicide occurs because the individual carries a deep belief that they are not loved and not good enough and, more importantly, they have forgotten that they have choice. The option to take your own life is then justified by the reality you create through fearful thoughts, derived from old harmful beliefs. On the surface, it is quite likely that a person can appear quite normal yet at the same time believe that they do not deserve to live. Of course everyone is different. What is quite evident is that our beliefs can be very dangerous to, not only ourselves but, those around us.

In my humble opinion, maintaining close relationships is the single greatest challenge, yet most rewarding pursuit, facing humanity. Relationships expose our belief systems up close and personal.

Our closest relationships are our most valuable 'mirrors' of who we really are and what we truly believe. It is difficult to hide those old unconscious beliefs in a close intimate relationship. We can conceal them for a time but at some stage, when your guard is down, those old chestnuts will come to the surface, generally to the bewilderment of your partner. This then provides a wonderful opportunity for learning about ourselves, and raising our consciousness.

So how do we know if our beliefs are working? Some of the following questions might help answer that.

Is your life joyous in every aspect? Is your day full of love and fun and do you live in an abundant state with perfect health and happiness? Do you love your job and jump out of bed each day in wonder at what wonderful experiences you will encounter today? Do you feel that you make a positive difference in the world? Are your relationships loving and open? Is your world a peaceful harmonious place? If not, then I would suggest that your beliefs are not serving you, unless, of course, you do not want a life of perfect health, wealth, joy, love and happiness. Think about that for a moment. Is your life what you want it to be?

The suicide bomber is only playing out their life in line with their core beliefs. You are no different. Everything that you bring into your life is a result of your thinking, and your thoughts are crafted by your core beliefs.

Some of those beliefs could be;

- Money is evil
- Nothing ever goes right for me in relationships
- Cancer runs in my family
- I am too old
- I never win anything
- I'll never get the job I want
- I could never possibly do that
- Its too good to last
- I don't deserve this
- People always let me down
- I can't make a difference
- I don't have a choice
- I am not good enough
- The world is not a safe place

Take time to write down some of your own beliefs that you are aware of, or should I say the ones you think you are aware of. Pay particular attention to the areas of your life that you are not entirely happy with and jot down your deepest thoughts about those areas. These beliefs could explain why you are not experiencing what you really want. Be totally honest. If you look deep enough you will find some doubt or fear driven belief there somewhere. There must be, otherwise you would have total joy in that area. Uncovering 'hidden beliefs' is a little more challenging and usually requires the assistance of a close friend or partner brave enough to be brutally honest with you. If you are up for it, then enlist their help. You might be surprised what you learn. Be sure to be totally open. Your source of feedback must trust that you will accept their opinion without reservation. They must feel safe to speak freely without repercussions. Just listen and ask questions. Resist the temptation to justify or refute their view.

If you can truly trust a close friend or lover, and allow them to give you an unfettered view about you, then you are on the path to self-actualisation. The receiving end of raw criticism can be an uncomfortable place to be for most of us. The process must be handled with care.

Some dear friends of mine, Terry and Barbara Tebo, created a self-help program called 'Free to be Me' a number of years ago. They have been teaching 'Free to be Me' for around forty years and conducted over 250 programs. The program is designed to challenge some of those core beliefs and how they impact our view of life. If you do not feel comfortable with a friend or partner challenging your beliefs then I strongly suggest that you seek out some professionals like Terry and Barbara with experience in that field. It can be a scary thing to learn what your hidden beliefs really are and having access to some support and guidance through the process can be comforting. Terry and Barbara have published a book titled 'Free to be Me' that I would recommend as good reading. Bruce Lipton also covers beliefs in more technical detail in his great read

"The Biology of Belief", or there are any number of other publications and practitioners that can help.

———

Business organisations sometimes use the 360-degree feedback process as part of their performance appraisal system. This can also be a very effective way of unearthing hidden treasure. Like any personal feedback, the success of 360-degree evaluations depends on the acceptance of that feedback by the individual being appraised (appraisee) in a positive manner, and also on the person providing the feedback (appraiser) being totally honest. And that means brutally honest. Remember feedback is only one person's perception and opinion. It is not the truth, just their truth. It is your own reaction to the feedback that provides an insight into your own beliefs. These feedback mechanisms must be carefully implemented if they are to be effective. The process is certainly not an avenue for disgruntled individuals to unload, although the actual feedback given can provide just as much insight into the beliefs of the appraiser as the appraisee.

The critical component of the 360-degree method, as it is with any personal feedback, is trust. The participants must all trust that their comments and responses are taken sincerely and not used against them. Similarly the appraisee must have the feedback download handled sensitively so as not to be intimidated by the process. If the participants have any resistance to this process then there is clearly fear at play and some positive affirmation and nurturing for their inner child is suggested before you even start. To be successful a robust and safe process is essential.

———

To change your behaviours you have to change the beliefs and attitudes that drive the behaviours.

Beliefs evolve over time and we have all changed a belief somewhere along the journey? One that comes to mind is the belief in Santa Claus. When you believe in Santa your life experience continues to deliver and support that belief. In the case of Santa Claus the gifts arrive every Christmas and are just what you put in your letter or, at the very least, what your parents could afford from what you put in your letter. Even when other kids at school told you that it was your parents that bought those gifts, and they just make the rest up, you just can't accept that straight away. Why would it not be true? Why would people you love and trust be deceiving you?

As I recall I was afraid that if I stopped believing in Santa Claus that the presents would stop. In fact that is pretty much what my parents told me. Looking back, what they said was the absolute truth. When I asked is Santa Claus real they answered 'as long as you believe he is real he is real'. That made little sense at the time but now I get it. This is still very relevant advice. What we believe to be true will be true for us while we continue to believe it, regardless of the impact it may be having on our happiness or health.

What you believe will be your reality.

As the old saying goes **what you believe you can conceive and will become reality.** In reality what you believe you **will** conceive. Henry Ford summed this up nicely - "whether you think you can, or you can't, you are right".

If you believe it is real it is real. No ifs or buts. However, there will come that time when you doubt some particular beliefs, such as when I caught dad wrapping the Christmas presents and I recognised the paper that mum bought at Kmart. Once you have accumulated enough evidence to the contrary your belief is no longer valid. Dad had been playing me along all this time. How silly I felt.

One of the major challenges facing humanity is our inability to let go of damaging beliefs. We live in the age of information and more and more new evidence is arising everyday that challenges old thinking. This is no more evident than with the medical profession where treatment continues along genetic lines and ignores the critical part played by thought and energy in the healing process, despite this being consistently demonstrated through the placebo effect during testing. I will expand on the placebo effect later in this chapter. While the influence of mega pharmaceutical conglomerates plays no small part in this 'cover up', it is our own inability to let go the beliefs emanating from our 'deepest fear' that fosters this deeply destructive aspect of humanity. We get so attached to certain dogma that our beliefs become us and we refuse to listen to any alternatives, instead following blindly. We think that what we believe is actually who we are.

What beliefs do you still have now, that if proven to be wrong, would have you shaking your head and saying 'how could I have ever believed that?' It wasn't that long ago that we were encouraged to laze in the sun because it was good for us to have a healthy tan. Now we are told no more that fifteen minutes and then to slip slop slap! We were told that smoking was good for us for goodness sake and we believed it! Smoking was fun and made our lives happy! Surely the advertisements could not lie? People used to believe that the earth was flat and we find that quite ridiculous now. I expect that within a few decades that people will look back on some of our current beliefs, such as drugs can cure disease or our job is more important than our environment, and think exactly the same.

If we accept that beliefs drive our thoughts, and thoughts subsequently create our reality, then it is incredibly important to adopt the beliefs that support the life that we want. If your life is not blissfully happy and contain all of the things that you want then I suggest that you could do with a refresh of some of your beliefs. If we want to change the destiny of humanity we all need a refresh of a number of our beliefs.

Hold your beliefs lightly.

I watched some re-runs of Men in Black recently. For those who have not seen this series of movies, starring Will Smith and Tommy Lee Jones, the storyline involves well-dressed government agents, in black suits, working with the secret service to protect humanity from a variety of aliens that inhabit a futuristic world. The agents have a fancy device called a neuralyzer, a bit like a camera flash in a pen, which is capable of wiping the memory from anyone exposed to the flash. Imagine for one minute that the world population was 'flashed' with that device. All beliefs and memories erased. How wonderful would that be? No one would be angry. No one would be sad or frightened. We would all just marvel at the beauty around us and seek to learn about our environment. The world needs a bloody big neuralyzer!!

To change a belief you need to come up with an alternate belief that you like, one that will serve you well, and one that you can firmly believe.

Of course, certain universal truth will still apply regardless of the reality you choose. In practice your own beliefs can never override the reality that;

1. Everything is connected (energy is the base component of the universe)
2. Spiritual life is eternal (energy can not be destroyed)
3. Our thoughts create
4. We have choice

An interesting characteristic of personal beliefs is that they are formed without the need for any evidence at all and yet, despite the existence of mounting evidence to the contrary, we vigorously defend them before we would ever consider letting them go. And all of this, despite the fact most of our deepest beliefs were accepted when we were children. That is to say, before any filters were developed, we simply took what was said, or what we experienced, as the whole truth. Those careless lines from a teacher saying that we would never amount to anything went straight in and, having accepted a belief, our ego will find every possible way to prove that it is in fact the truth. We will attract the evidence we need to support the belief rather than seek alternate evidence, and experience, around us to challenge it. I believe that my immune system is strong and perfectly equipped to heal any ailment. I get evidence all the time and my belief is reinforced. I know others that believe that they can never be wealthy and guess what … they get that reality.

The propensity of humans to hang on to, and defend, old beliefs is at the root of all human conflict.

To change a core belief is not always as easy as we would like and may take time, just as my letting go in the Santa Claus example, despite having ample evidence to the contrary. While changing beliefs seems difficult it is really as easy as making a conscious decision to do so. During my recovery from depression the kindness given to me by my son, in that compassionate hug, activated my awareness and revealed some pretty damaging beliefs that I had been carrying. My decision to change was pretty instantaneous. It was as if a bright light was turned on in that dark place where my fearful beliefs were stored. The process from there certainly required a sustained effort but my intent was clear, strong and immediate. I have had many doubts along the way but always managed to bounce back. Some call these immediate eye-openers 'ah ha moments'. I just love 'ah ha' moments.

So how do we change those old beliefs? Firstly you must choose what it is that **you want to believe.** How do you want your life experience to be? How do you want to feel? When you know all that then make a daily practice of meditating on these beliefs, reinforcing them in every cell of your body. The secret is you have to believe it. If you do not believe you can fly then don't bother trying to download it as a core belief. You personally have to truly believe it is possible. It is a bit similar to choosing which apps you want on your electronic device. You have thousands to choose from but which ones do you really want? Of course, if your apps become out-dated, or simply no more fun, you can delete them quite easily. The same principle applies to your beliefs.

I strongly recommend that you research a methodology called PSYCH-K, developed by Robert M Williams. You can Google the website for more details. This method works at a quantum level and has achieved some amazing, and often immediate, results in changing damaging subconscious patterns and beliefs. On the basis that, at source we are all vibrating energy, then it makes perfect sense that this energy can be reprogramed provided we are open to change. Update your operating system. You do on your computer to stay relevant so why not your own human hard drive?

Until you have fully assimilated your new belief you will likely need to 'fake it until you make it', or pretend you have changed. This is not so much about ignoring the emotions that arise, that are contrary to your new belief, but rather acknowledging them and knowing that they have originated from thoughts not yet in line with the new you. Despite the same old emotions and fears arising, maintain that you have changed already. Remember the old memory, or pattern, has over time formed neural pathways in your brain and until some new pathways, or patterns and beliefs, have been well established your default pathway will continue to be the first accessed. That will become more natural once you have directed a few 'hikers' onto that new track. This is quite ok. Your new awareness will allow you to disengage autopilot and take control. You can get back in the drivers seat. That is what faking it actually is. It is not ignoring your feelings. It is exercising choice. It is choosing to create the life circumstances that you want.

You can change your life by choosing to act and think consciously different thoughts, despite experiencing emotions and feelings that may not support your endeavours.

I have read stories of people that believe they can walk through walls and, quite frankly, if they truly believe that they can, then who is to doubt that they cannot. After all, matter is only vibrating energy and more space than substance, so why not indeed? Of course if your own belief system does not accept walking through walls as a possibility then it isn't going to happen is it? I am ok walking around walls for now.

I believe that I create my own reality. I believe that I am connected to everything that exists in the universe. I believe that love is the most powerful energy in the universe and the core essence of universal energy. I believe that I make a difference. I believe that my immune system is strong and that I have the power to stay as healthy as I want to. Because I believe these things, I continue to get evidence of them every day of my life. If I believed that everyone was out to get me then I would attract all the evidence that supported that belief. Mind you, I still have the experience of hidden beliefs every now and then and I certainly still have a reflection in the mirror!

I know it sounds too simple and if it was that easy then why isn't everyone doing it? That is a great question. Remember, "Our deepest fear is not that we are inadequate. Our deepest fear is that we are powerful beyond measure". It can seem daunting because it involves taking personal responsibility for all aspects of your life.

It is often more comfortable for us to blame outside circumstances, seemingly beyond our control, and accept mediocrity than it is to accept that we do have the power and take responsibility for our life situations. This does not mean we all have to follow in the footsteps of great leaders. You can practice taking responsibility for your life at any level, either as a parent, as a partner or any ordinary person. The choice is yours.

I expect that some of you are thinking, this is all well and good but I want to see some evidence, as in in the Santa Claus story, that my old beliefs are not enhancing my life? You don't need proof. I will explain further in chapter nine when I expand on acceptance. Ultimately, your proof will be the joyous life that you experience.

While you seek proof you have doubt and while you have doubt you do not have belief. If you doubt a belief it is not yet a belief.

During that transitional period following the downloading of a new belief, fake it until you make it. What you feel is real, is in effect real. Eliminating doubt takes intent.

———

We create our reality through our thoughts and our thoughts are driven by our core beliefs. It then follows that it is not possible to have an outcome that is not perfectly in line with what we really want and believe. How could you get cancer if you did not truly believe that you could, unless at some subconscious level, there is doubt around this belief? Absolution from cancer is a perfect example of damaging beliefs in action. Mainstream media, and the general population, are fearful of cancer. The belief in cancer exists in the collective consciousness. Cancer is big business. The single biggest beneficiary from the belief that cancer does not exist, is you. Many huge corporates, medical professionals, technology giants, drug companies and even corporate charities exist wholly because of the widely held belief in cancer. That belief will take some unwinding but, in truth, the body has the perfect mechanism for handling rogue cells and viruses – the immune system and of course our own belief system. We just have to believe it and let it do its job. Cancer is just like everything else, created from thought.

It is my view that illness and disease are not caused by something outside but are a direct result of a lack of something within.

The magnitude of human thought, and media hype, in relation to cancer makes it a daunting challenge for any of us to hold a belief that it does not exist. Yet there are any number of amazing stories of people diagnosed with inoperable terminal tumours that have completely healed without the use of drugs or radiation and, in some cases, **despite the use of drugs and radiation!** How is that possible?

The power of our beliefs to heal is best demonstrated through the placebo effect. The placebo is a sugar pill, or benign remedy, that is used in conjunction with the scientific testing of new medicines or treatments. Consistently large numbers from test groups, unknowingly given the placebo, continue to record similar healing outcomes to those who are given the actual test drug. The reason for the outcomes is that the individuals believe they are being treated and the body responds accordingly. Major drug companies conveniently dismiss this phenomenon as part of an acceptable error rate.

Unfortunately, no real investment into the reasons behind the success of placebo healing ever happens. After all there is no money for corporates if you can heal yourself **without side effects** is there? I personally doubt that drugs have any real affect at all and that all of the real healing is from the belief that they do work.

Undoubtedly, it can be challenging to adopt new beliefs. I have known many people that talk superficially about holding certain beliefs and yet their behaviour does not support what they say they believe. Spiritual people claiming they believe in the Law of Attraction, and taking responsibility for their own creation, yet when things do not go according to plan they are quick to blame an external factor. We all have a tendency to revert to our old subconscious beliefs when under stress, or in times of adversity, hence the value of awareness and the emotions that bring this to our attention. A person's behaviour is always a better way to determine a person's true beliefs, rather than what they tell you.

At times of high stress there is a window into a person's real character and belief systems. Stress can make us behave differently from what we have in the past. Stressful situations are the best time to observe people and see what they really think, and thus believe.

I can cite a real example of this from a corporate experience in an Australian credit union. This business had established a living culture and passion for what it did. The business valued its people and their role in delivering its vision. The business had the highest staff engagement score that I have seen. The Chairman at the time had a mantra that "its all about the people". He was an extremely popular and approachable man. The business was in the process of transitioning to a more sustainable economic model, due to the Global Financial Crisis, and when the incumbent Chief Executive retired the Board chose to appoint an accountant, from a public service background, as his replacement. I will expand on this a little more in chapter thirteen. While the consequences of that appointment are still playing out, I can tell you that the dynamic staff culture has all but been destroyed and morale is almost non-existent. The Chairman of the Board, when alerted to some specific behaviour of new Chief Executive, clearly not in the best interests of the people, was more concerned with an improvement to the cost to income ratio than the morale of the staff. I learned at that moment what the true beliefs of the Chairman were and about how actions, and not words, determine what one really stands for and believes.

So lets have another look at how to change a belief.

The first step is to identify the belief you want and document it into a written affirmation. Lets for argument sake say the belief you wish to reaffirm is that 'I create my own reality'. This is a great one because it is in alignment with the universe. Start to research the topic. There are many great authors on this subject or you can scan the Internet to uncover more supporting information.

Write it down. This action carries great power. Keep it visible. Read it daily and most of all feel it at all levels of your existence. Intelligence is located in every cell of your being. Do not get trapped into just thinking. I suggest that you assimilate your new belief in a quiet place, free of interruptions, or on any break where you get a quiet moment. I generally work on my own affirmations just before I go to sleep. This allows the new or boosted belief to integrate overnight. First thing in the morning, before my mind starts buzzing with other thoughts, is another perfect time for affirmation. If you are struggling to come up with a suitable affirmation, respected self-help author, Louise Hay, has some particularly powerful examples in her material. Louise Hay also suggests there is strong evidence that speaking the affirmation at your own reflection in the mirror has greater impact. Of course if you have no reflection then you have no need for affirmations in any case!

Repetition of your new belief will eventually replace past programs as your programs of first choice. The more hikers on the new path the better marked the trail! Of course, past programs have been in place for a long time and will not go quietly. Do not get discouraged if you find yourself slipping on occasions. Change takes commitment, determination and intent. If your vision of a new you, and a new life, is strong then your determination will be strong and you will succeed. All you have to do is believe that you can.

It is essential that you live your new belief by staying present. Feel the experience of life and observe your new belief working. Look for the evidence that you need to support your belief all around you. Believe it is happening. Observe others. Listen to what they say and what drives their reality. You will get working examples everywhere you go. Heightened awareness is vital. Try your best to be present and watch those doubtful, damaging thoughts that will surely surface. Smile and let them go.

Persistence is vital. This is the rest of your life we are talking about here. A blissful, harmonic, joyous, abundant, healthy and loving existence is surely worth some persistence.

Do not resist. What you resist will persist. Change at this level is about implementing new programs and beliefs and NOT about denying old programs. The old beliefs will still be around for a while so let them go gently. You must forgive yourself and forgive others. We are spiritual beings living a human existence. Part of that human existence is that we make mistakes - a timely peek in the mirror, to check for a reflection, will remind you that is true. Our whole purpose is to experience and by making mistakes we learn. Resist the temptation to judge.

If you slip or fall or lose it, for goodness sake give yourself a break and forgive yourself. Shake yourself off, have a laugh and go again. It's that simple.

Life is not meant to be serious. Seriously!

Chapter 7

THE POWER OF
THOUGHTS – YOU ARE
WHAT YOU THINK

As I pointed out in previous chapters, thoughts are the very first step in the creative process. Our thoughts create. That being the case, and thoughts having so much power, we are all no doubt very mindful of what we are thinking, right? Well we should be.

At this point I would like to make a quite selfish declaration. I am writing this book for me. Why, well I am connected to all of you, as well as everything else that is, and our combined thoughts are making my world, and probably yours, a potentially unhealthy place to be. Every unconscious act is slowly poisoning both you and me. None of us are removed from the consequences of destructive and fear based thoughts. While I am personally comfortable with the concept of death, I would add that I am really enjoying this physical life and I want to continue to live it in peace and harmony. The point is, we all benefit when we think and act consciously. We all need to be much more selfish and think of what is best for each of us. When I say thinking of us, I mean 'us' as in the greater us that is the wonderful organism of vibrant life we call earth. Our greater self is in fact our environment, our earth and our universe for that matter. Every loving conscious thought and act we perform for ourselves is done for all of us. Conversely, every negative unconscious act or thought directed at us impacts everyone else as well.

What are you thinking right now? I mean what are you really thinking? As you focus on that question you will bring attention and awareness to your thinking and you will, most likely, experience that the random thoughts that were there a moment ago have now dissipated and your thinking is focussed on what you are thinking right now. And that should be 'what are you are thinking right now?'

Does any of that make any sense to you? Never mind, now that I have your attention...

The point is, while we are not focussing on what we are thinking, the mind is randomly generating literally thousands of thoughts, of which we have very little awareness. When we focus on our thoughts we can actually halt our thinking. Try for a minute just waiting for the next thought to come. Waiting, waiting... no thought. By focussing our attention, our conscious awareness is in control and the ego is silent. In this state we are actually totally in the present moment and thought is not possible in a true state of presence. Sure, it probably won't take long for thoughts to start up again but with practice you can extend the thought free period. Achieving a thought free state is a core principle of meditation. The aim is to cease thought and be totally present. In that moment of total presence the true power of manifestation is accessible. From that conscious state it is possible to control our thoughts and direct them toward creating what we really want. A highly conscious being lives life predominantly in the present moment. If you think about it, nothing really ever happens anywhere else but the present anyway. Anything outside of right here and now is pretty much just thought about past or future. Thoughts about the past generally generate guilt and those about the future, fear. Conversely the right here and now is the place where unlimited possibilities and truly joyful living reside. There are no problems in the present moment because there are no thoughts.

Researchers estimate that the average human being generates around 70,000 thoughts per day. If that is anywhere near correct then some degree of care is in order, don't you think? Do you remember all of your thoughts from yesterday? I certainly do not. The great majority of these thoughts are randomly generated from below our level of consciousness and pretty much pure nonsense; well at least I think they are! The only real way we have to check what type of thoughts we have been generating is to observe where our life situation is right now. How are we feeling and what is our level of happiness, joy and pleasure. You can trace those outcomes directly back to how you have been thinking in the past. Thoughts create remember.

What you experience now is simply a result of what you have been thinking in the past.

With that wonderful thinking machine, the mind, running amok and randomly creating our material world, is it any wonder that the planet is in chaos. We have over seven billion people generating on average 70,000 thoughts per day! I don't have enough characters in my calculator to give you the total number of thoughts but I can assure you it is a lot. The thing to remember is that the great majority of these are random and unconsciously generated. The good news is that while most of this thinking makes little sense, unconscious thought has less power than focussed, conscious thought. When I say that subconscious thought makes little sense, I do so because it is not thought from a conscious rational source, but rather our ego, and is distorted by our hidden beliefs and subsequently impacted by fear.

I will explain that further by using the concept of the inner child. I consider the inner child an aspect of our ego. The inner child is the part of us that carries the fears of our childhood, and the part that wants to eat more chocolate when you know full well that you have had enough. Like any child, our inner child likes to have fun but can also harbour deep fears from the experiences of growing up. This part of us needs a lot of 'TLC', or self-love, to keep us emotionally healthy. While I may seem to be painting a picture of the ego as a major source of pain for each of us, and our planet, the ego is an essential part of being human. It contains our personality, although we should always remember it is not truly who we are. It gives us the experience of being individual and different even though we are all one at source. As human beings we should embrace this child within us, as we would any frightened child, to make it feel safe and free to play, and enjoy the fullest life experience possible. In my experience when you have a happy inner child you experience a happy life externally.

_____

Much of what has happened in the past has absolutely no relevance to us in the present. Well it should have no relevance in the present unless, of course, we hold onto those memories and they influence our beliefs and thinking now.

I liken the ego mind to owning a powerful luxury motor vehicle. Lets imagine a twin turbo; V8 supercharged red Porsche (we all know that red goes faster) sitting in the driveway. This is an example of the power of the mind and our thoughts. This marvellous machine is capable of amazing high-end speed and outstanding performance. This is state of the art motoring perfection. However, to deliver amazing performance, it has to be driven. It will not perform all that well sitting in the driveway. Someone has to drive it. Now imagine that machine on the road at high speed with a seven-year-old child driver. Imagine the absolute chaos! At best the result would be widespread damage and it could be potentially fatal. May I remind you that the mind can produce similar carnage when the uncontrolled thoughts of our ego are at the controls? Should you ever experience the sense of your mind racing you can now appreciate this is not a great thing, unless you are in the drivers seat. A racing mind can be very dangerous and destructive.

In my own experience of depression, my unrestrained ego was having a ball tearing around in that machine. I was racing down the highway of life with absolutely no control over that monster. Before we all panic and conjure up images of a major freeway catastrophe, I should put this into some perspective; some thoughts carry more power than others.

True creative power comes from passionate thought fuelled by emotion and feeling.

For a thought to carry any real power it has to be felt. Most of our randomly generated, nonsensical thoughts do not get the supercharge effect of our feelings because they are generated without intent. It is when we get a repetitive pattern of thought, creating emotion in our body; we know the engine is running. That generally uncomfortable, clammy feeling is the rumble of that mighty V8. Best get hold of the controls quickly. If you are feeling emotions then the mind is running.

Pay attention to your emotions. When emotions are in play someone has started the Porsche!! You have a choice to hop in and go for a spin, by being conscious of your thoughts, or alternately let it loose without a licenced driver. It is your choice but beware - choices have consequences.

If we have access to such a fine machine why not use it? Why not indeed. As with any high performance vehicle, before you are able to extract maximum output, you need the right driving skills and experience. Yes, just like everything in life we need to learn some stuff first. The unit of competency for conscious creation, or 'conscious mind driving', is learned through meditation. Meditation is the practice of clearing the mind of thought, being present and allowing space and clarity for the driver to take the controls of the Porsche, rather than the damn thing driving itself. Deliberate thought, validated by emotion and feeling, puts you in the driver's seat and is also the basis of the effective use of the Law of Attraction (creation). You simply have to be paying attention to your thoughts.

Now this is the tricky bit. The process of conscious creation is not the difficult part at all. All of us create all the time. Just look around you. You created all of it, your life situation, job, relationships, personal belongings, where you live, health disorders and so on. You did that. Take a bow… or not. The potentially scary part is you most likely did it unintentionally. I call that process 'random creation' which is what we witness in humanity today.

To create intentionally you will need direction, some sort of a road map or GPS.

For any journey we need a map or an annoying digital voice from our GPS. "Take the second exit… perform a U turn where possible" - give me a break! Seriously, without a map and a planned destination we would simply drive around in circles, get lost or at best not end up where we really wanted to be. Does this have any relevance in your life? Are you at your perfect destination? Do you feel that you go around in circles sometimes? I know I still do. The map is the critical part of conscious creation. I should point out there is absolutely nothing wrong in just driving and exploring. Life is about the journey after all. My point is, if you want to get somewhere in particular then you must have a destination in mind.

*To create what we want **we must know what we want** and that ladies and gentlemen is the most challenging part of the creative process. Knowing what you really want.*

What do we really want? Where do we really want to be? Can we ever really know what it is we really want? The answer is certainly yes, we can know what we want, but *that does not necessarily mean that any of us know what it is we really need.* What we need is intrinsically linked to our higher self, that part connected with universal intelligence. I believe we get the experiences we need to raise our consciousness for the benefit of all of us. The chaos all around us on planet earth is clearly delivering a range of experiences comprising wonderful learning opportunities. The chaos on earth reminds us how we can do better and be more conscious in our actions. It has certainly inspired me to write this book. The point remains, on planet earth, and in our daily lives as material beings, we still have the power create our own desired outcomes by focussing our thoughts.

The throttle for creative thought lies in our feelings; the universe knows the best route. Forget about the process, the universe is our spiritual GPS. However, only we can really know where it is that we want to go. We have to enter the destination! This is a basic principle of goal setting. It is okay to seek divine direction, which is akin to leaving creation to fate, and it is also ok to use imagination. This means leaving it to the universe to guide us to where we should be. That works for many but you must keep your thoughts under wraps otherwise hidden fear, from old beliefs, will be the unintended guide and not the universe at all. It also pays to be fuelled up on passion. Passion is produced from the core belief in your journey. Passion fully engages your whole being.

Passion boosts creative performance.

While we do not always know *how* to get to where we want to be, we should know *where* it is that we want to be. We must provide the destination, described as clearly as we possibly can, in our vision and, more importantly, be clear just how it will make us feel when we get there. This feeling part is essential. The universe will follow the universal law and deliver and attract exactly what we put out for, based on the energetic vibration of our thoughts and feelings. It will not create anything outside what our thoughts and feelings request. We will of course be required to take some inspired action, and make certain choices along the way. There will be many signs and opportunities. Yes, there will be lots of signs and choices along the way. The universe communicates with its own GPS directions. These are not a voice saying, "Take the second exit", but rather a feeling you get; does this feel right for me?

The process I have described above is very much that of traditional goal setting. I currently facilitate a sales program for an Australian leadership development company, Leadership Management Australia (LMA). At the core of their program is the concept of personal goal setting. Goal setting has been around for a while, although I am not sure that everyone gets the connection with the Law of Attraction and the power our thoughts play in creating outcomes. The steps to effective goal setting are pretty much as I have just outlined;

1. Be clear what you want and how it feels to have it
2. Write it down in specific language (SMART*)
3. Have belief
4. Take appropriate action and make choices
5. Use affirmations to build confidence (fake it until you make it)

*SMART is an acronym for Specific, Measureable, Attainable, Realistic and Tangible.

The founder of the LMA parent company was an American entrepreneur Paul J. Meyer. My favourite quote of Myer's is "Whatever you vividly imagine, ardently desire, sincerely believe and enthusiastically act upon, must inevitably come to pass!" It all starts with knowing exactly what you want.

Now that reminds me of a little story of the man who put out a vision of losing weight. He wished and wished to quickly lose fifteen kilograms. That was his sole focus. He just wanted the weight off. He did not care how. He meditated and meditated and focussed solely on that outcome. Sometime later he developed a thyroid condition that increased his metabolism and stripped the weight off him in a matter of weeks. This also required that he go onto specific medication to arrest the condition. Vision delivered?

Be careful what you ask for and for goodness sake be absolutely clear about how you want to feel at your destination. Using the Law of Attraction is all about the feeling that you want to have when you get there. In this case the feeling the man was most likely seeking was one of feeling better in his body and having an increased level of fitness and energy. That does not necessarily require a quick loss of fifteen kilos. The point I am trying to make is, had his focus been on that feeling of good health and fitness that he really wanted, and then he applied resolute intention on that feeling, he would have been presented with a way to arrive at his desired destination in perfect health and wellbeing. I should point out that I might well have made this story up. Or did I?

Once we are able to experience the feeling of being where we want to be, in our own individual reality, we are actually already there.

Life is simply a matter of perception. If you feel wealthy then your bank balance is irrelevant. I would imagine that Rupert Murdoch would feel pitifully poor if he were down to his last million dollars while others would feel like kings with a thousand in the bank. It is all determined by what we believe, think and feel.

Most of us want to attract money. Money is a great example to use to explain the importance played by feeling in the creative process. So you want to be rich? Well if this creative thinking thing is any good I should be able to win the lottery, right? Wrong! As I indicated before, being wealthy is a feeling and not an amount of money in the bank. It is all relative remember. If you asked me how to create a million dollar bank balance I would ask you how you wanted to feel. Why do you want to attract this outcome? After drilling down to the real reason, a typical answer may be 'the freedom to do what I want and help the people I love'. That is a noble goal and one that can certainly be aided by having money. However, the outcome is not entirely dependent on having money at all. That outcome is a feeling. Rupert Murdoch may not feel he has the freedom to do what he wants with a six figure bank balance yet you may feel completely free and able to help your loved ones with much less. It is all a feeling and the Law of Attraction is based on the vibration from your thoughts and feelings.

Money itself is just paper we exchange in lieu of love and gratitude, nothing more and nothing less. Without ego, our true spirit would have no purpose for money. We would give to others out of love and be grateful for the opportunity and others would do likewise.

To get the feeling you want you might have to 'fake it till you make it'. Imagine having achieved your vision. Feel that you have it right now. Be grateful that you already have it. Thank the universe for what you have. Use affirmations to support your feelings and to defend against any sabotaging thoughts that will certainly arise from your unconscious bank of negative beliefs. How do I know that you have some negative beliefs in your subconscious? You would already feel wealthy if you didn't. It's really that simple.

Don't worry about the how, just dream about the having, and feel the feeling of genuine gratitude from the having, right now.

The diagram opposite is my own map of the Law of Attraction or what I prefer to call 'Conscious Creation'.

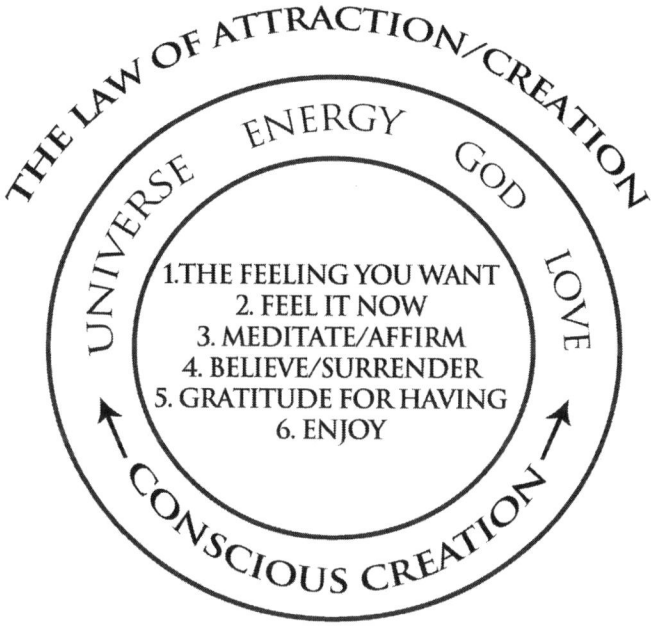

The outer circle contains the ingredients required for Conscious Creation and represents the loving, energetic intelligence that makes up our universe. This vibrating, energetic stuff makes up everything and therefore knows, and is, everything. The inner circle contains the order of conscious creation. Start with the feeling (goal or destination) in mind. Be crystal clear in how you want to feel when you get there. Fake it till you make it and feel the having of it now. Clear any fearful thoughts and focus your intent on your desired destination by using affirmations to support the feeling of being there now. Believe, have faith and surrender to the process. Be thankful for already having the feeling you want and enjoy it now. Why wait? Once you believe you have reached your destination you are already there.

Perception is reality.

So armed with a map (the vision of what we really want and how we want to feel) and sufficiently skilled (consciously aware of our thoughts) we can now safely, and with confidence, take the Porsche for a spin on life's highway - without running some poor bugger over. And remember, it is a journey and not a race. While a focus on the outcome (feeling at the destination) is an essential part of the creative process in our human existence on earth, life is all about the journey. Enjoy the ride, smell the roses and absorb the beauty of the scenery along the way. Oh and of course lookout for signposts, and pedestrians.

There will be many signs that offer different choices along the way. Feel what is right for you and if you take a wrong turn then you can always take another route or choose another destination or "perform a U turn where possible". There are no rules in that regard. It is simply a wonderful thing to be alive so enjoy every moment of it.

Chapter 8

JUDGEMENT – EVERYONE IS ALWAYS RIGHT

For much of our lives we find ourselves either on the receiving end of judgement or handing it out ourselves. In fact human society is geared up with rules, regulations and interpretations that encourage us to make a judgement and label actions as either right or wrong.

In chapter six I explained that our perception of reality, and consequently our judgement, is derived from our unique view of the world as seen through our own filters. We label an action based upon our view of reality, as determined by our beliefs, and therefore our judgement is not necessarily relevant to any one else. We generally make judgement on behaviour we are unable to accept.

To judge is to not accept.

The universe has a set of laws that in turn apply to us as a connected part of the universe. One of these is the Law of Attraction, which works closely with the Law of Cause and Effect. Often referred to in Eastern cultures as 'Karma', the Law of Cause and Effect is a simple law with simple principals.

Every action has a consequence. Sir Isaac Newton's Laws of Motion broadly encapsulated this universal law along the lines that 'every action has an equal and opposite reaction". This law sits nicely with the notion that we are creating our own reality. Each and every energy emitting action, including our thoughts that are forms of energy, will create an outcome and deliver an equivalent response or consequence somewhere else.

So it seems to me that the universe already has consequences built into life so what is the purpose of judgement? Why would it serve any purpose to place a right or wrong label on any action when universal laws already determine an appropriate consequence as part of universal process? Additionally, do humans need to have separate laws if the universe already has them?

It seems pretty obvious to me that our current human existence, which is dominated by mind driven egos, cannot function without a set of 'human laws' and procedures. The human ego experience is basically a game and we all know that games must have rules or no one will play nicely. Unfortunately, those setting the rules are often doing so to directly benefit from the game and powerful lobby groups influence government policy. It stands to reason that once the mind is engaged, and a vast array of realities are coexisting in our 'society', there has to be a standard set of rules that apply to all. As parents we call these rules boundaries and these boundaries must apply to everyone within any group to hold relevance. Each country, state, municipality, village, religion, business and family may have a different set of boundaries but we should remember that this is purely a human phenomenon. These rules are required to manage egos in a predominantly unconscious society. Of course when rules, between say religions and countries, are at odds the result is confusion all round. You do not have to look far to see examples of that happening!

At our current level of consciousness we also need to apply man made consequences in relation to certain actions. When you consider the bigger picture of humans simply being a part of a larger living organism (earth) this all seems a little superfluous, don't you think? I do. God must be laughing out loud (lol if he had a Facebook page) and, as we are in fact pieces of God stuff, we should be laughing at ourselves. Hey life is meant to be fun after all! It is ok to laugh.

Many ancient civilisations had customs and ceremonies that were much more aligned to universal rules. Australian Aboriginal culture, as an example, respects the people's affinity with the land and the concept of stewardship rather than ownership. Aboriginal people understood that they were only looking after the land and their survival depended on doing just that. Ownership was not a part of their custom. Unfortunately, we now find that humans will do almost anything in the pursuit of ownership as it makes them feel safer. It sounds to me like the ancient Aboriginal custom makes much more sense and would serve us well right now. How can the concept of ownership exist in light of quantum evidence that all is connected and everything is a part of everything else? How can you own a part of yourself that is in quantum reality also a part of someone else? Surely custodianship is a much more realistic way in light of quantum reality?

Judgement does not exist in a highly conscious environment. It has no place in nature and absolutely no place in the function of the universe, which already has laws that apply as part of just being. Herein lies the problem. Man is actually a spiritual being having a human ego experience and as such is bound by universal laws. However, man is also governed by a separate set of man-made rules and boundaries developed to appease the ego, with the consequence of generating judgement.

Spirit does not judge. Judgement is a concept of the ego.

So is judgement wrong? Well that requires a judgement. Judgement is neither wrong nor right it is simply unnecessary outside the world of human ego. Remember that judgement is not about consequences, as I will explain further in chapter ten. The secret to a life of joy and abundance, without fear, is found in remembering your spiritual link with the universe and its laws of being. As functioning members of society we all have to accept that judgement will be applied to us under the human system, but we must also know that judgement is not real. Try not to use it yourself. Accept what is and live and let live.

This does not mean that as leaders and individuals that we will not be required to make decisions based on human laws and policies because we surely will. While we should never forget that we are actually spiritual beings (connected vibrating particles of universal God stuff) we also exist in a predominantly unconscious material world. In this material world we have the power to create whatever we want. In this material world we are able to make choices and in this material world we will face material consequences. Until such time as every human on this planet has evolved to a state of high awareness and consciousness there will be a need for human law, process and consequences. That does not necessarily mean judgement!

Let me give you a personal example. My home is located on the Pacific Highway in the lovely seaside tourist village of Urunga in New South Wales. The township is located at the juncture of the Kalang and Bellinger Rivers where they merge before emptying into the mighty Pacific Ocean, on the stunning east coast of Australia. The town is in the process of being bypassed as a part of the Pacific Highway upgrade. The Pacific Highway is the major road linking Sydney and Brisbane. Yes I have a very busy driveway. One morning I was on my way to Coffs Harbour, about thirty minutes north of Urunga, for a business meeting. I was running a little behind time and was still enjoying my piece of peanut butter toast, crunchy of course. Not the complete health food breakfast but very tasty nevertheless. As I entered the highway I dropped the delicious morsel onto my lap. Because I was running a bit late, I was no doubt generating some random, unconscious and negative thoughts. I unbuckled my seat belt for a few seconds to remove the offending toast from my trousers at the very same time as a NSW Police mobile patrol passed in the other direction.

I had refastened my belt by the time the police car had completed its u-turn at my driveway and raced up behind me to pull me over. I explained to the officer what had happened and why my seatbelt was unbuckled for those few seconds, where I lived and how close my driveway was, which he duly verified during my licence check. Despite now being even later for my business appointment, and feeling more than a little annoyed, I was quietly confident that the officer would see my indiscretion as very minor and send me on my way. Wrong! The bugger wrote me a ticket. At the time I was not all that impressed with the nature of events and I made some pretty blunt judgements about the personality of this policeman. But you know what, he was only doing his job and making a decision based around a set of human rules. Who was I to judge him?

When I looked back on this later, and my emotions had subsided, I realised that my negative thoughts had actually created the situation of running late, with the consequence of eating my toast as I as driving onto the highway, with the consequence of the toast falling in my lap and so on.

In a more highly conscious state my day would have flowed very differently. It was only my thoughts that created the chaos and applying judgement only deepened my angst. As soon as I let go of judgement I was back at peace with the universe and could laugh at my situation. Mind you when the $225 fine came up for payment several weeks later I did have to go through another letting go of judgement exercise! Can you believe that? A fine of $225 for three seconds! Oops there I go again.

This example does serve to highlight the challenge in applying 'unnatural' human laws that achieve sensible outcomes. The officer felt my actions were against the law, which in the strictest terms they were, while I saw no possible harmful outcome to anyone. Who can best judge which interpretation is right? While I still feel some degree of flexibility was in order, upon actually reading the written law it is quite clear that it is an offence to 'be in a moving carriage without a secure seat belt fastened'. That seems fairly black and white. The officer did not really need to make a judgement. He had the facts and I admitted that my belt was off for a few moments. He just followed procedure, without a high degree of consciousness mind you. Doh, there I go again.

An earlier version of me played Australia Rules (AFL) football. When I found the impact a bit too stressful on my body, I decided to take up umpiring the game and eventually coaching other umpires for a number of years. I am still involved at a local level. I just love blowing the whistle and making decisions. The last time I read the rulebook it had about eighty odd pages, incorporating many individual rules that must be interpreted by an umpire. During the one hundred odd minutes of an AFL game an umpire may award around thirty free kicks or penalties and, if you include the times when the umpire makes a decision not to award a penalty, the decision-making and judgement calls are well into the hundreds each game. While a rulebook is written in black and white, also the colours of my favourite AFL team Collingwood for those that care, the interpretation is not always that clear.

What I found enormously helpful was a pamphlet the AFL produced titled "The Spirit of the Laws". I found this an extremely useful tool when coaching. This brochure explained in simple terms the purpose of the rules, for instance to keep players safe. The spirit of player safety covers a number of regulations, such as bumping and high contact, and gives the actual rules a purpose. Consequently, while an umpire must still make a judgement call they are doing it with a view as to why the rule was implemented in the first place, rather than just the wording of the actual rule itself. The interpretation then becomes more meaningful. Umpires must also assess the intent of the players. Were they trying to take possession of the ball or were they trying to inflict injury on an opponent? Decision making can become quite intuitive after a while. You can essentially feel what a player is thinking, not that they will always agree with you.

We seem to have lost sight of that original intent and purpose in our legal system. There is a strong case for having a similar 'Spirit of the Laws' for police and judiciary to remind them what the original intent was behind the legislation. What was the original intent when the seatbelt law was introduced? Was it safety? In that case what was the safety issue with me at my driveway? Just saying. I have let that go by the way!

Judgement has no place in a highly conscious world. However, until such time as our consciousness evolves, our laws, procedures and guidelines must be crystal clear. The more clarity the less need to apply judgement. If statutes and policies are clear, well communicated and have clarity around the consequences in the event of breaches, we are then able to make informed choices. There is little need for judgement when laws are clear. Remember a judgement is an opinion based on one's own beliefs, which explains why we see such variation in consequences under our laws. These variations are no more evident than in the different laws in different cultures for drug offences.

The political debate, both in Australia and abroad, in the lead up to and following the executions of two Australian drug smugglers, by Indonesian authorities in 2015, was incredibly heated. This was despite the laws having been widely known and legislated for many years. Regardless, there will always be individuals willing to roll the dice and try to smuggle dangerous drugs in and out of Indonesia, based on the potential monetary reward if they do not get caught.

Individual beliefs got a thorough public airing when the executions were to be enacted. Andrew Chan and Myuran Sukumaran were convicted back in 2005 and were reportedly rehabilitated by the time their execution was carried out around ten years later. Mainstream and social media were inundated with opposing views and judgements regarding the actions of the Indonesian government and the offenders. Visitors to Indonesia are clearly warned, with large visible signage, that the death penalty will be applied for drug smuggling. The country takes a much dimmer view on drug use than most western democracies. The policy is not a new one. Indonesia has executed many offenders previously with little media uproar from Australia in the past. The extremes of public feedback demonstrated how each of us is influenced by both our own individual beliefs, and by any close relationship we may have to the parties involved. Some clearly see no use for the death penalty, regardless of the crime, while others consider it is a strong deterrent and sure way to prevent reoffending. Either side can logically argue the validity of their position. That is the way of human judgement and beliefs. There is no real winner. We are all right. The consequences of drug smuggling were clearly defined and communicated by Indonesia and yet, upon implementing the decreed punishment, our moral judgements come into play.

Likewise, when setting policies in a business, or indeed boundaries in a family, it is important to clearly define the consequences, the original purpose why the policy was created in the first place, any tolerance factored in, and the measurement method. These factors should all be stated in the policy and the policy owner must ensure that those subject to the policy/law know about it. There is no real option to exercise true choice if the consequences are not known before the choice is made. In the event of a breach the need to apply a judgement is reduced. There may be a factual investigation as to the details of the breach but the need for judgement is diminished. Any penalty is then only a representation of the evaluation of the data. In the case of my seatbelt offence there was no tolerance but I have let that go. Or have I?

Of course those of us with children have been faced with the dilemma of enforcing boundaries, and making judgements as to the right level of consequences for our child's behaviour and actions, or indeed lack of actions. Its not easy but without clear consequences, and the intent to enforce them, you will make a difficult time of it for both yourself at home, and your children when they eventually face the outside world and its countless rules and laws. A clear explanation as to why the rule exists is the key. If the rule cannot be linked closely to a purpose, and that purpose is not valid, then the rule should be scrapped. A perfect case in point is the compulsory use of helmets on cyclists.

This one is a pet gripe of mine. What is the purpose of making adults wear protective helmets while riding their bikes on quiet suburban streets, through a park or on the beach? The creators of this ridiculous law would probably say personal safety. Selective statistics will show that just as many people sustain head injuries from tumbles and falling tree limbs, while walking or running through parks, as those on bikes. There are those who, upon being alerted to those pedestrian statistics, would push for a new law making helmets compulsory for walkers, whereas I would argue for the right to exercise personal choice and accept the consequences. There may be a case for wearing a helmet while riding on the highway but on the beach and off road, really? Clearly there are two different sets of beliefs at play here? I will always support personal choice, provided the consequences are clearly understood.

When evaluating the enforcement of any law or policy, weigh up the facts and make an assessment in line with the original purpose of the law. This will minimise the need for judgement. The definition of right and wrong is, after all, an individual interpretation. We are always right. We all see reality through our own unique filters, coloured by our own beliefs, most of which we have little understanding in any case. While we have differing beliefs systems in the world, there will always be disagreement about enforcement or non-enforcement. Bearing that in mind, it would be futile to impose a right or wrong judgement.

There can never be full agreement where different beliefs exist.

The best we can do is to agree on the policy or law, understand why it exists and ensure the consequences supporting that purpose are in line with the likely consequences to those offended by a breach of the law. That is, apply an equal and opposite effect, as much as that is possible. The purpose is the most important consideration. Communicate it clearly.

Being right or wrong will always be a matter of perception based upon belief.

Chapter 9

ACCEPTANCE – STAYING PRESENT WITH WHAT IS

Acceptance is a highly conscious behaviour. Accept what is and you will be surprised how much less stress there will be in your life and on our planet. What you resist will persist.

Acceptance is often the most misunderstood concept of all. Acceptance is not about giving in, or putting up with inappropriate behaviour and circumstances that are threatening or unsavoury. Acceptance is certainly not about continually living with what you do not want. We all have choice and an ability to change our circumstances. However, to make a change you must first accept what you have and where you are right now. As leaders, parents and human beings we all have to accept what is, before we can start to imagine how we would like it to be.

You can't begin a journey without knowing and accepting exactly where you are now.

One of my greatest lessons has been letting go of my need to understand how things work and why they exist. As a Virgo male I have always had a thirst for knowledge and a tendency to analyse things to death. I just wanted to get to the bottom of stuff and find out why. I found it difficult to integrate new information unless I fully understood the reasons behind it. I must have driven my parents absolutely mad, and a boss and teacher or two along the way. Just do it Rod – yes but why sir? Of course having understanding is very useful when dealing with practical matters, such as problem solving or a Sudoku puzzle. Did I tell you that I am just slightly addicted to Sudoku? I find it a fantastic way to exercise my brain and keep my analytical thinking sharp. Some who know me well might suggest it is not working that well, but I digress. There is no doubt that problem solving, in a material sense, requires a high degree of understanding about the subject matter, and process, to be effective, but not all things follow logic.

I have come to appreciate in my later years that when it comes to more complex matters, such as love, relationships or intricate concepts such as infinity and life itself, trying to reach an understanding is just a waste of valuable time and energy. In fact I have reached the conclusion it is practically impossible to understand some concepts. For example, how the universe works, what happens after death or the concepts of infinity and love. I am not saying that people cannot have a view and be able to communicate their perceived understanding as to those matters, but I very much doubt that a full understanding exists. Any explanation is just an individual perception and tainted by the usual environmental factors that contributed to the formation of that individual's own filter.

Relationships have been a particularly fertile learning ground for me. I had spent so much time and effort trying to understand intimate partners that I almost went crazy. A wise friend once said to me 'Rod you do not need to understand women, you just need to learn to accept them". That was a big ah ha moment for me. Of course, why rack my brain for understanding when the solution is about my heart being able to accept. How can a man expect to understand such complex ideas as the infinite universe or women? How can a man expect to fully understand himself?

I had a belief that understanding was an essential ingredient for a full and peaceful life. I can assure you there is absolutely no need to understand anything when you learn to accept everything. That is not to say that you cannot learn more about such intricate matters, such as love. The learning, however, will be through the experiencing. My advice to those seeking a peaceful life would be to drop any expectation of ever fully understanding and start accepting.

To practice acceptance you must learn to appreciate that there is only ever one moment - the present moment. The future is a moment that has not yet happened and the past is a moment that has already been. We only ever have the moment we are in to take any action and derive full joy and happiness. I found that seeking understanding was a thinking process that took me out of the moment. Acceptance resides in the present moment. There is no happiness in the future. When you finally get to the future you are actually in another present moment. If you are continually waiting on the future to deliver happiness you will always be waiting because the future is merely a concept of the human mind. It does not exist. In fact it could be argued that the future is the very same present moment that we always have been in. Therefore, the future can only ever be experienced in the present. Eckhart Tolle describes this concept beautifully, and in a most detailed fashion, in his popular book 'The Power of Now'. This is one of the most influential books of my life experience and potentially a generational changing publication. If you have not read this book, and want to know more about this topic, then I strongly recommend that you get a copy.

Once you can master acceptance you can overcome the resistance to what it is that you are not accepting. Your life will then flow more in line with the universal energy of unconditional love. To not accept what is happening right now is to resist what is. That is not to say what is happening right now is what you want to be happening right now but guess what, it is happening right now and the only responsible thing to do is to accept that it is happening right now. From that place of acceptance you can make choices and instigate change.

Humans spend a lot of time complaining about their lives. From their bank manager, politicians, health, jobs, kids, spouse, among numerous other things. It is an interesting experience to walk up to someone and ask him or her "how are you doing?" In my experience the answer is often a negative one like 'no bloody good' or 'could be better' or 'same old sh#* different day' or even 'you don't want to know'. Well I do want to know and that is why I asked. I am often tempted to respond with 'so what are you going to do about that?' With my friends I am likely to do just that and

I have also been known to stun a young checkout attendant or two with the same question, when they have complained about the sad state of their lives. I do get some crazy looks, mind you, but the fact remains humans are inclined to default to negative responses. We are either worried about something that has happened or something that might happen in the future. A person in the present moment will not be worried. They will feel alive and grateful for what they have right now. They will take appropriate action and exercise choice if they want to change something, but they will not complain, because in the present moment there is absolutely nothing to complain about. They will accept what is and they will respond accordingly.

Lets look at a couple of scenarios that might explain this a little better. Imagine that you are walking through a park alone one evening when several seemingly intoxicated and disorderly characters approach you and rather aggressively ask you for money. To ignore them is not a real option. The first thing is to accept what is happening. I am alone and I may be in danger. This is not what I want but this is what is happening. From a position of acceptance you can take appropriate action in the present moment. Fear will serve no purpose. Fear will only cloud your awareness. Depending upon your size and athletic performance you could choose to defend yourself, or retreat at a fast pace to a safe distance. Alternatively, you could assess this as a low danger situation and engage in dialogue with the prospective offenders, or indeed you could just hand over your money. From a perspective of balance and acceptance you do have options. It is obviously not an option to simply ignore the situation and pretend it is not happening. You must accept what is happening right now. To resist would likely result in an internal dialogue along the lines - 'why is this happening to me' or 'I'm going to die'. That thought process leads to fear, limited choices and worse. Remember the power of your thoughts.

I liken this to what happens every day when we pick up a newspaper, or turn on a television, and are confronted with another brutal murder or political blunder and just shrug and think - 'this world is pretty well stuffed' - and go about our day as if nothing as happened. The point is that the world is not stuffed! We are only ever one thought away from a new reality and, from a state of total presence, everything is perfect.

Thoughts do not happen when you are totally present. If you are thinking about an action you are no longer totally present. The best being and living happens in the present. Being and thinking are opposites.

The same applies in less violent situations where there is no immediate need for action. This could be in a relationship where your partner has an annoying habit that drives you absolutely crazy. For instance, let's say constantly leaving the toilet seat up after using the bathroom. I will make the assumption that the partner in this scenario is male. I will admit, as a male, I have struggled with this one but I have learned that it is a very important issue with Venetians. If you are the aggrieved partner then the first thing to practice here is acceptance. The non-acceptance of this habit will only lead to anger, stress, frustration and all the discomfort that goes with those emotions. You should also note that your emotions are arising from thoughts impacted by your own beliefs. If you accept this situation is happening right now, then you can make balanced choices. In this scenario some choices that you could make include;

- explain to your partner that you would like the seat put down after use
- put the seat down yourself
- remove the seat altogether and leave it on your partners pillow
- go to your mothers for a week
- learn to live with the seat up
- replace your partner

Having accepted the situation you can make balanced choices without the interference of high emotion. Naturally choices have consequences. In an emotive state your reaction may not bear relevance to the event. This is what happens with road rage and toilet seat rage.

Acceptance is not something that comes naturally to the ego. The ego is in fear of its own existence and run by thought emanating from a flawed belief system. Acceptance is similar to detachment in that detachment, from an outcome, is a form of accepting. Success comes from focussing on the immediate task at hand and not the outcome. Detachment should never be confused with indifference, which is basically ignoring what is happening. Indifference is not a state conducive to making good choices and will eventually lead to consequences down the track. Indifference is not a healthy, or loving way of being.

Like most things we learn over time, it is only through practice that we improve and eventually become proficient. When I say proficient I mean well trained, not perfect, and still with a mirror image. Acceptance is no different. Every time you are feeling a strong negative emotion, such as anger, frustration or anxiety, it is most likely because you are resisting something. Stop and go deep within to find what it is that you are resisting. It may take you a while to get down through the layers but keep asking, why you are feeling this way, until you get to the source. Once there, you can then accept it is ok to feel that way, forgive yourself, and return to the present moment where all is perfect. From the present moment you are able to take the most appropriate action, which may well be doing nothing at all.

I find that driving in peak traffic is a great way to learn to practice acceptance. Some days I do better than others! It is important to monitor your emotions, as they are the body's way of letting you know that your thoughts are not in line with the universal energy, and that you are resisting something. Stop and identify the point of resistance. Lets say it is the slow driver in the 100 kpm speed limit that was only a moment ago doing 110 km in the overtaking lanes as you pulled out to pass them. You are now in single lanes where you cannot pass and you have a conga line of drivers lined up behind you also getting frustrated. You are on your way to work and running a little behind for an important appointment, or you could have screaming children in the back seat. Sound familiar? Remember, this driver is not driving slowly to personally annoy you. This is about you and your reaction to an external event, NOT the other driver. Your frustration and anger is a result of your thoughts about being late (future), or why does this always happen to me (past). This is a great time to practice acceptance. After all, you have plenty of time. You can't really do anything else but work on changing your attitude and getting back into the moment.

The first step is to block all of those thoughts that are flooding through your head. Take deep breaths and think peace and calm. Send love and understanding to the driver holding you up. Perhaps repeat to yourself something like "I am so grateful for this opportunity to practice acceptance." Resist the urge to imagine your hands wrapped around the other driver's throat. Remind yourself "this is about my reaction to an external event not the other driver". Shift your attention to what is happening right now. What are you feeling? What is happening around you? Be conscious of your thoughts and engage your whole body by becoming aware of your total physical presence. Focussing on full body awareness is a great way to ground in the present moment. You could sing along to the radio or just admire the scenery. Do keep an eye on the road as well.

This may sound ridiculous but I can assure you that driving in slow traffic is a much better situation in which to practice acceptance than in the heat of a domestic dispute with your partner, or a volatile meeting with work colleagues. You will get better at it. That is what practice does. The more frustrating the situation the better the lesson to be had. You can now thank your partner for leaving the toilet seat in the raised position. What a wonderful teacher your loved one is.

The value of accepting what is happening, and not reacting, is that you will remain present and, in the present moment, fear does not exist, the ego is still and clarity and choice are accessible.

A person truly in the present moment is focussed, clear and connected. A person truly in the present moment has the ability to make the best possible choices and decisions. As an individual, or indeed a leader, the present moment is where you want to be as often as possible. Accepting the 'what is' is a window into that present moment. Any resistance to what is happening, or what has happened, will prevent you from being present. If confronted with a situation and you feel your emotions rising (remember that emotions are telling you what you have been thinking) and you want to be clear and focussed then firstly, breathe. Feel the emotion. Focus on what is happening right here and now in your whole body. Being anchored in your body will settle the mind and ground your presence. Feel all of the sensations. Focussing your attention on the whole body will also help stop the flood of thoughts that have created the emotion in the first place. It will keep you in the present.

Our natural tendency, through ego, is to be overcome by thoughts. What has happened? What does this mean? What am I going to do? Who did this? Why does this always happen to me? Watch a professional tennis player, or golfer, that is having a bad day. Their talent has not diminished from ten minutes previously; their thoughts have taken them away from the present moment. Stay present. Observe and ask questions for more information, if you need to, but do not race ahead or go into judgement about what has happened. The answers are always available in the present moment. Stay with it. The ego will be persistent. Your emotions will be simmering. You may feel uncomfortable. The unconscious mind will seize the opportunity to revisit all of your deepest darkest beliefs and doubts and pour out fearful thoughts into the universe. This is an ideal time to assess your capacity to stay in a conscious and present state despite all of the chaos going on in the subconscious mind. This will reveal how well you can control your ego. This is when you need to be firmly in the driver's seat of that red Porsche. This is the time to take control of your responses, accept what is happening, and calmly engage the shift of that fabulous V8 (mind), gently of course.

It may also be a good time to repeat some well-rehearsed affirmations, in your head, to bring you into balance. I say in your head because others around you may react oddly if you say them out loud. If the situation is simply too volatile, and other egos are running rampant, then it is often better to leave the situation and defer any decision making until you feel settled and totally present, if that is indeed an option. Take time for reflection. These potentially stressful situations are perfect times to learn about ourselves and grow our own consciousness. Decisions made in haste, when emotions are high, are invariably decisions that you will regret at some time in the future.

In my experience, most of the very bad decisions that I have ever made have been made at times of high stress and volatility, when influenced by emotions created from fearful thoughts and beliefs, although some have also been clouded by alcohol. I am sure that we can all think of a time, when with hindsight, we would have acted differently to how we did. Being present is very much like having hindsight in advance. Being present enables us to feel into the decision, often referred to as having that gut feel, and limit the impact of uncontrolled and indiscriminate thoughts.

Higher consciousness can be experienced in the present moment and in that moment everything is perfect and you will know what feels right to do.

Chapter 10

CONSEQUENCES – EVERY ACTION HAS A REACTION

I touched on the theory "Every action is attended by an equal and opposite reaction" in chapter eight.

When Sir Isaac Newton penned this law of motion he observed that "if one object exerts force on another object, then the second object exerts an equal and opposite force on the first".

While the application of this theory has been somewhat superseded by Einstein's Theory of Relativity, and more recent quantum discoveries, the principal of Newton's law can still be broadly applied to human society, in a similar way to Karmic Law. Whether it be leading our own lives, or impacting the lives of others in a defined leadership role, it is essential to accept that consequences exist as a part of nature. Nothing happens in isolation. Every action will set off an equal reaction somewhere else. That assumption is still just as relevant in a world of quantum energy as it was when first written over 400 years ago. Everything is connected and all actions are felt across the entire universal energy field, in some way or another.

We know that our universe is made up of vibrating energy, all things are connected and thoughts create our reality. Thoughts are also vibrating energy. Thoughts lead us to actions and manifest outcomes in our material world. In effect what we think and believe will determine our perception of the world. What we think and do has consequences. There is an equal and opposite reaction at a vibrational level. We will, at some level, reap what we sow. These beliefs are at the core of the concept of taking personal responsibility.

Lets look back at the structure of life. On the one hand we have an infinite universe that is made up of vibrating light energy (God stuff), in perfect harmony and balance. What sometimes looks like chaos is actually governed by simple basic universal laws and more complex mathematic formulas. This universal blueprint is best exemplified in nature. When I say nature, I mean nature in the wild, without the interference of man's thinking. Everything is in balance. There is no fear. Death is accepted as a part of life and the whole environment of plants, earth, water and animals exists in perfect harmony, despite the occasional calamity of drought and flood. Sure some animals eat others, and yes some animals fight each other, but only as part of the natural behaviours that support the survival of that species. In that environment the planet flourishes. All is in balance.

On the other hand we have this tiny spark of universal consciousness, we know as human life, that has developed a low level of consciousness (that's us). This tiny morsel of consciousness is able to experience through complex receptors within its brain and cellular makeup. A life form able to experience separation from the universe, the very same universe that it is in truth just a part of, and feel that experience as an individual experience, and totally different from all others. I refer to this as the ego experience. This ego experience is governed by fear. The ego believes that death is the end and it will do anything to avoid death, including taking another life. The ego will try to control its environment, destroying nature to protect its own growth, all the time believing that it knows more than the universal energy from which it is created and that it is in truth, still very much a part of. Welcome to planet earth.

This may make the ego sound evil, and in truth the ego has the capability to be quite destructive and evil. However, I have also suggested that the ego also has a number of different aspects, including the ability to play, dream, imagine, laugh, lust and care. To destroy the ego entirely would be akin to the experience of human death, which is basically the return of the human spirit to the universal pool of life. Many humans make the choice of death to avoid the ego experience and its seemingly unending fear and turmoil. Suicide rates increase every year. While this is an alarming statistic we must also accept that each individual has choice. The sad thing is that suicidal people do not always understand they do have choice, particularly where negative thoughts have taken over and the individual has no awareness of, or in essence forgotten, who they really are in truth. I have been there. The ego can be mighty dangerous when it has the controls of the red Porsche, believe me.

The real joy of a human life experience comes when we balance the ego experience with the truth of who we really are. From that point of balance humans can be a part of the natural flow of nature, and consciously contribute to its survival. In that state of perfect balance we would not fear death and we would appreciate the biological cycles by which nature is bound. We would remember that we are in truth spiritual beings having a human experience and that, while the laws of nature will govern our bodies and subject us to the cycle of life and death, our spirit is eternal.

Humans have an inherent propensity to be both compassionate and greedy creatures. Man is capable of forgiveness and kindness but also entirely selfish behaviours. Humans believe that they have control over outcomes without consequences. They believe that they alone can determine consequences by way of human laws and systems. Over time, man seems to have forgotten the law of cause and effect and the phenomenon of karma. These laws continue to apply regardless. To ignore these universal laws does not in any way decrease their relevance. The consequences will apply regardless of whether we choose to believe or not. Remember these universal truths are not negotiable. Just like gravity with our trapeze artists.

Nothing happens in isolation. We are all connected to everything.

In a highly conscious environment consequences would be completely accepted as a part of being. Consequences would have no judgement attached. Consequences would be seen as a natural part of our existence. In fact in a highly conscious society, people would exercise free choice and happily accept the consequences. People would make measured decisions before they made choices, based on a set of possible and likely consequences. There would be no regret because all actions are taken consciously. No appeals, no excuses, no "I didn't mean it" or "I was having a bad day". Wow, how simple would that be! If I choose not to wear my bicycle helmet and I fall and cut my head then so be it. Conversely if I happened to be fined by an overly attentive policeman for not wearing my helmet then so be it, although in a highly conscious society there would be no need for such a law.

If we observe nature in the wild, we see consequences in perfect balance. If the hungry lion catches the gazelle then the gazelle becomes the meal. If it does not catch the gazelle it goes hungry. If lions become super successful at catching gazelles then the lion population grows and the gazelle population dwindles. The consequence of that happening is that the lions have less food to catch, they starve and their population reduces and, as the lion population decreases, so the gazelle flourish once again. The balance of life is maintained. All is in perfect harmony. Consequences are in perfect balance, just as the universe intended. Nature does not have anxiety or use judgement. Nature just exemplifies life and the natural consequences that come with living on planet earth.

What we are experiencing in our world at present is humans trying to manage consequences. We are making judgements as to what the consequences should be while other ego-based minds do whatever they can to avoid consequences all together. These actions run contrary to universal laws and will, and do, have other 'unintended consequences'. The energy of the original action will create an opposite and equal reaction somewhere else. Think of this in terms of pouring a one-litre container of paint into a container half the size. The extra paint has to go somewhere. It will not just disappear, it will run until it finds a place to settle and have an impact on that place. That could be on your beautiful new carpet! Nature has equilibrium factored in. It stands to reason that applying human consequences, from the perspective of a material ego mind, can never work in nature as we are physically a part of it.

If we accept that everything is connected, then in effect an individual avoiding a consequence in truth means that another part of the 'all', which may well be in the form of another individual, will suffer the consequence. Ultimately, as we are all connected, we all experience the consequences in any case. The paint will run on to the carpet or somewhere else. This is demonstrated in cases where violent criminals are released early on parole only to reoffend with even more violent crime. Perhaps the original consequence was not commensurate with the offending action? I hear human rights arguments from both sides of that scenario, and yet this sort of imbalance continues to exist.

Until such time as our race elevates to a level of consciousness where we can live an existence from pure love, the need for man made rules and consequences will still be a necessary part of human life. However, we simply must get better at assessing the relevance between actions and consequences. As parents, employers or friends, we will all be faced with this choice at some time in our lives.

To assist someone avoid the consequences of an action is a futile exercise and will simply transfer the consequence to another part of them and you.

Effective laws and policies have clearly stated consequences that are well documented enabling individual awareness of those consequences. Of course there is no point having clearly documented and known consequences if they are not enforced. If we are to get anywhere near some balance with the natural laws of karma operating at a higher level, then man made consequences must represent, as best they can, an equal reaction to that of the original action. The Bible mentions 'an eye for an eye' and perhaps this is to what that phrase is referring, although it is possible to attach any number of different meanings to biblical quotes. So who decides what consequences are appropriate and does that mean a life for a life? These are both great questions deserving of a better answer than I could ever provide but great questions that deserve an answer none the less.

If consequences are in any way to relate to physical laws, it stands to reason that the force or intent behind an action should dictate the force or intent of the reaction or consequence. Newton's law is about the force of an action being equal to the reaction. I would imagine that an actual premeditated action carries a lot more energy than a spontaneous action but how can we ever possibly measure that? Is it any wonder that we have such inequity in our laws. We will never get this right until we are all living in our naturally higher conscious state of love. It just doesn't make any sense otherwise. In that state, of pure loving consciousness, we would never need to evaluate consequences. The universal laws in place are already perfect and we would accept them.

The death penalty is a divisive subject. I mentioned this in regard to the executions in Indonesia. We know that if the consequence of an action is not commensurate with the energy and intent of the original action then there will be carry over consequences occurring somewhere else. There has to be. I must say that I get a bit confused when, as a society, we can live with the unintended casualties resulting from a premeditated decision to bomb a terrorist group. That could include the inadvertent killing of innocent civilians, including children, as 'collateral damage' yet at the same time we are unable to apply a death penalty to a known brutal murderer who can never be safely released into society.

Death is simply a part of the life cycle and only a transition after all. While the concept of death as a transition, and not an end in spiritual terms, is quite valid, the reality of taking a human life is very challenging to accept when faced with actually making that choice. Yet, as a race, we continually make conscious decisions to go to war and consciously kill our enemies, most of whom are simply following orders out of fear. The world of the ego is never simple is it? It can never make sense because of all of the factors influencing our individual realities.

Behaviours and actions taken to avoid, or lessen, the natural consequences of the original action are, in a holistic sense, completely pointless and will result in unintended consequences elsewhere.

The reaction, or consequence, has to be at the equivalent level to the initial action to avoid unintended consequences. Remember, this law will apply regardless how man may try to interfere. Our world is continually impacted by the unintended consequences created through our inability, or unwillingness, to adequately apply equal and relative penalties to the original action. We have a system that preserves the life of multiple violent murderers, at massive financial and emotional cost to society, while at the same time we are unable, or unwilling, to afford to feed starving children and protect vulnerable lives. Unintended consequences? We continue to expand the extraction of coal and oil because it is purportedly cheaper (I will challenge that assumption when I address the 'true cost' methodology later in chapter fourteen) to run our cars and makes the balance of payments look better, when we know full well that fossil fuels are poisoning our very existence. Unintended consequences? We bully and intimidate individuals because they dare to be different to us in their beliefs and customs when in truth none of us are right and all of us are right. Unintended consequences?

What about the unintended consequences of love?

The good news is that there can never be too much love or compassion. It is simply not possible to love too much or be too kind. As the universal intelligence that created us is also characterised as pure unconditional love, the only possible impact of putting out too much love is the expansion of the power of the universe. Positive, loving and compassionate actions and thoughts replenish and nourish us all. Can ending a life be a compassionate and loving act? It is all about the intent. Our immune cells do not get angry when they eliminate an infection. This is purely an act of love for the benefit of the greater organism.

In the workplace, an event of manifestly uneven, either harsh or weak, consequences will have unintended consequences for the culture of the business. I see that all the time. Whether it is soft action against a bullying manager, or an over reaction against an employee for a minor misdemeanour, an inequitable response will carry over somewhere else with consequences for the organisation, and its stakeholders. The cost, both in financial and emotional terms, is not clearly understood by many business leaders. For instance a business that has a model of fear-based management will attract and retain people that respond to fear. That is, they will not take risks and will not be creative because they are frightened of the harsh consequences of making a mistake. The job seekers that are creative and confident will either leave, or not even apply for a position with a business driven by fear. Management then falsely believe they have their staff under control, which they perceive as a good thing. On the surface this approach may appear to reduce conflict because staff are too frightened to speak up. In reality, however, good employees just leave. Management would hardly notice - "they never did what they were told anyway". This narrow sighted approach fails to appreciate the consequences on business performance in having a fearful employee pool. Passionate, creative people, with the courage to face fear and take risks to achieve outcomes, are successful people, the types of people you want in your organisation. These people will not stay in a business run by bullies.

If we delve a little deeper, the concept of consequences for actions gets even more interesting. Science can measure an action of force but we have not evolved to the stage where we can measure the energy of an action of thought or intention. How then do we get an accurate consequential balance? Only the universe itself can do that and it is already factored into the fabric of creation. All man really has to do is get out of the way. But we are not ready for that just yet and in the meantime it all comes back to what feels right in the heart. This whole topic of fairness is only relevant in an unconscious world in any case. If we all took more responsibility, and accepted that we are all connected, would we still take actions that harmed another part of us? If we can all be a little more compassionate, and open our hearts a little bit more, we can turn the tide.

The solution comes back to raising the consciousness of the entire planet through each of our own actions and thoughts. When that happens there will be no need for punishment because our actions will be conscious and from the heart. Such actions are then from a level of unconditional love and purely intended as a benefit to the whole, and the consequences are even more love and understanding of each other.

It is important when responding to a situation that the ego is kept in check. Stop thinking and feel what is the best reaction, in the knowledge there exists the potential for unintended consequences, and that love heals everything.

Chapter 11

Values in Action – What do You Really Stand For?

A key responsibility for leaders and individuals in a highly conscious world is to live and uphold a set of values.

*The values of a business, and of individuals, represent the principles as to **how** things are done and are derived from the purpose, or **why** things are done in the first place.*

Goals and objectives are meaningful tools and guide us to achieve amazing outcomes but clearly, from my observations, our governments, businesses and many individuals lack a solid set of values that they passionately uphold, and adhere to, <u>at all times</u>. I personally believe you can put that down to a lack of purpose. Purpose is the 'why' we exist and do what we do.

The end has never in the past, nor can it ever in the future, justify the means. It is more important how we live our lives than what we do.

To purely focus on result is to take a narrow material view of the world and is the way of the ego. To ignore the why and how is simply operating from fear, greed and control and quite frankly, just another way of avoiding personal responsibility. Always was and always will be. Unfortunately, corporate and political behaviour is typified by short-term, result driven behaviour and the world suffers accordingly. As I explained in chapter ten, when examining consequences, at a spiritual level you can never abdicate personal responsibility. As a connected society, world and universe there can be no winners and losers. If one part wins then another part must lose. Only outcomes achieved in the interests of the whole will serve both you personally, and/or your business, in the longer term.

At a macro level we all benefit or we all lose.

There is no greater example of high result, low values driven behaviour than that of legendry American cyclist Lance Armstrong. You would have to have been living on another planet not to know about the systematic cheating that Armstrong employed to gain success, wealth and power and the painful demise of the legend when all was exposed. The Armstrong way was one of intimidation and control. That is the way of the fearful ego. How many people knew what was going on and stood by? How many were too afraid to speak up? What does all that success mean to Armstrong now or to any of his followers, sponsors and teammates? The consequences are still flowing to Lance Armstrong. He recently lost a landmark fraud lawsuit that resulted in him having to repay $US10 million to a promotions company. More is to come with the US government expected to sue for an additional amount, expected to be around $US100 million, as a consequence of his cheating. Unfortunately for Lance, as an individual, he has not yet taken the opportunity to come clean and accept personal responsibility for his actions. He has a wonderful opportunity to use his story for so much good yet he continues to lack real awareness and maintains that he acted responsibly because others were doping at the same time. Regardless, the Armstrong story does provide a fantastic learning opportunity for us all and I for one thank him for what he has done. What were the values of Team Armstrong? Their actions would suggest the only thing valued was winning at all costs and in any way possible, and certainly that the ends justify the means.

Values cannot be measured against what others are doing. Values are measured against what you believe. Your true values will always be demonstrated by the actions that you take.

What are the real values of a business or government? It is certainly not the neatly framed statement on the office wall, or catchy election slogans. Values are demonstrated in what really happens and how the enterprise operates. Anyone can dream up a set of values for a business, and indeed themselves, to live by. Most businesses will have a set of values and politicians will swear to some sort of oath, generally containing value statements but as individuals we very rarely take the time to document what it is that we really stand for. There is an old and very pertinent saying that "you must stand for something or you will fall for anything". Unfortunately, we see this demonstrated in practice by individuals, corporations and governments that consistently fail to live by a set of meaningful values, instead chasing short-term rewards. As Jerry Maguire would say 'Show me the money'.

Why is it so difficult to stick to our values? I would suggest that those that do not live by a set of values are simply living from the head and not the heart. The head can pay lip service to principles and integrity, treating them as a part of the game. Conversely, the heart is connected to what is happening and respects what feels right. The heart is in alignment with love and the connected universe.

To mean anything, values have to be adopted like core beliefs. If you do not truly believe in the value of say transparency, then don't document it. If you do document it, then be it. Before committing to being transparent you need to fully understand what being transparent actually means and what the consequences will be. Without doubt, this is the most important step for an organisation or individual. What does this value look like in action and am I prepared to live by it? If you, with hand on heart, cannot commit and believe in the value then you will never live up to it. Over the years, I have been involved in strategic planning sessions with a number of organisations and the setting of values is always a challenge. I generally find the board and executive to be very passionate about the business values at the time, but quite often the implementation and measurement gets little attention afterwards.

If you are going to live by values then you must have measures in place to monitor performance. In the case of transparency it would be essential to measure each individual in the business, and the organisation itself, against that value for it to get any real traction. That could mean at board level each board member fully and honestly disclose any potential conflicts of interests that may arise during deliberations, while at the level of the receptionist, they would fully and openly participate in team meetings and the 360 degree feedback of their supervisors.

You also need a reason why you would want to operate transparently. Lets have a closer look at that. A quick search in Wikipedia informs me that transparent behaviour "implies visibility in contexts related to the behaviour of individuals or groups" and relates to openness and accountability. How would our world look if every individual, government and business were completely transparent in the way they behaved? Imagine that they were a model of absolute openness and honesty. That would flush out a few conspiracy theories! There would exist a level of accountability seldom experienced. That would mirror nature.

I personally do my best to lead a transparent life. Admittedly, I have in the past spent time as a less that open human, but I make a conscious effort to be real, and no more to others than what I actually am. I believe that being open and transparent is a self-accepting way to operate that avoids resistance and stress. The same applies to business and politics. In a highly conscious world everything would be done transparently, as occurs in nature. The lion does not pretend to be a zebra. You know what you get from a lion and you know the likely consequences from approaching one. Can you say that about your local elected member or your supermarket? What do they really stand for? You know what they tell you they stand for. Generally, that is whatever will be the less controversial option, or the most popular, or basically what they think you want them to say. But who are they really? What does your hairdresser really stand for? Would you choose their services if you knew that they abused their children? What if they smoked pot at home or watched porn at lunchtime? What matters to you and how do their values compare to yours? You can exert influence by choosing where you conduct your business and give your support. Where you choose to shop, and whom you choose to deal with, says a lot about your own values.

In a highly conscious environment there would be no judgement but there are always consequences. Consequences are built into the fabric of the universe. There would be no need for privacy laws because nothing needs to be private. Highly conscious people are forthright in their values and beliefs, they accept who they truly are beyond body and ego. In a highly conscious environment there is unfettered access to information and people are able to make conscious decisions and choices. Having a higher consciousness does not take away your choice to have fun and experience what you want. In fact it enhances those possibilities for fun. After all there would be no fear of doing, or saying, what you really wanted. Just consequences. You would, however, do and say those things in the knowledge that everything is connected and that every action has an equal reaction with consequences somewhere else in the universe that will ultimately impact you. As a highly conscious being you would, of course, act from the perspective of love and the consequence of love is more love.

Lack of transparency impacts our ability to make conscious choices.

We are, all of us, microscopic yet integral parts of universal intelligence and, as a result, we have access to all of the information that exists and, consequently, the knowledge to achieve any outcome that is in alignment with the best interests of everything. When our egos are still and we are totally present we can access that information through our intuition. What feels right will be right. That 'gut feel' can be accessed in the absence of fear and will not fail you because that is the feeling of connectedness.

Our evolution to a higher consciousness will be supported by some common values that we could all practice right now.

- We value all life equally
- We accept our connectedness to all things
- We take personal responsibility
- We value forgiveness
- We act from compassion and love
- We respect personal choice

Quantum science reminds us that we are connected to all that is and, as a result, we are a part of all life that is. If we value our own life then it follows that we must value all life. It is all or nothing.

If you do not respect all life then in effect you are not respecting your own.

———

What is ultimate truth and does it even exist? Individual truth is coloured by our beliefs. Ultimate truth is what I refer to as "that which we know to be true at a level of being and in the absence of the ego". If you let go of ego, cease thought and completely surrender to the present moment, you will get access to who you really are beyond physical body. From this state you can access your intuition and know what feels right. From this place you can accept what is, feel compassion, easily forgive and have access to what is ultimately, truth beyond ego.

Forgiveness and compassion are intertwined and uniquely human values. Both are acts of conscious humans and come from the heart, not the head. Compassion is purely an emotion of the heart. Compassion is the difference between conscious humans and the animal kingdom. Compassion is the desire to alleviate another's suffering without personal gain. A highly conscious society would abound in compassionate acts. Compassion is considered the greatest virtue in all of the major religious traditions. The Koran begins 113 of its 114 chapters with the verse "In the name of Allah the compassionate, the merciful". So how have we lost our sense of compassion for each other and our planet?

Compassion is an act from the heart and the heart is our connection to spirit, or universal God stuff. All living things have a degree of awareness. Awareness could be said to be physical in nature. Compassion, on the other hand, is an act of consciousness and consciousness is spiritual in nature. How did we lose our sense of compassion? We think too much, that is how. The thought-based ego, with its multitude of individual belief systems, is creating the chaotic reality currently being experienced by the majority of mankind. We have simply forgotten who we really are.

We have the capacity to make personal choices every day. Whether it be what we read, what we eat or what we think. It is easy to get swept away with our life situations and treat that experience as being real. In fact our life situation is no more than a dream. As I explained earlier, our minds process stimuli from a minute part of all of the information that is available, and then sifts that data through our own filters, to give us a unique interpretation of what is happening in our lives. Our life is no more than our personal perception of that limited information. Our dreams are no less real than our lives. Have you ever had a dream that felt exactly like it was happening? Your heart is racing and you feel that you are really somewhere else. That is all life is, a waking dream!

Athletes use visualisation in a similar way to dreams. They basically simulate the race in their minds before the actual event. Sport science has found that a visualisation, in the mind, will exact the same physical responses in the body that would be stimulated during an actual race. The body believes it is real. Life is like that. What exactly is real and what is not? Reality is simply what we believe it is and we know that we can choose our beliefs. Just as we can choose our beliefs so to can we choose our values. If we can choose what to believe and value, then why would we not choose what is in the best interests of us all. Surely that is no more than we would want from others?

A conscious individual or business will stand for values that are in alignment with their responsibility and purpose to the universal energy that created them.

Conscious people, and business, act in alignment with their true purpose and measure their success against their purpose with as much vigour as they would measure their financial performance. They consciously choose how they act and respond. They consciously support other businesses, and individuals, with similar values. They do not judge others as right or wrong, or better or worse. They operate from the heart. They accept this way of being and living as a personal choice. You alone have the power to decide how you want your life to be lived. You alone have the power to choose which businesses you want to work for, or support with your custom. And you alone have the power to support the political candidate or system that you believe is authentic and conscious. Your own personal values and beliefs make up, and impact upon, the value system for the whole planet.

The cells of our body have no conscious control over their own beliefs. They respond to the very same beliefs stored in our subconscious minds and react accordingly in support of, what they feel is, the wellbeing of the entire body. The living cells of the human body respond to the instructions (thoughts) of the mind. Not all of those thoughts contribute to the health of the body and in fact often work against the health of the body. Cancer, anxiety, stress and many other diseases occur that way. As individual humans we all contribute to, and make up, the greater consciousness of the planet. Collectively we have the power to influence the global belief system and therefore dictate the health of the larger organism, earth. Remember the power of the hundredth monkey. Each and every conscious and loving act makes a difference and moves us closer to that 'hundredth monkey' tipping point. It is a numbers game and all of us count. Every human cell must work joyously together for the expansion of life on a healthy planet. This task may sound daunting but that is only because "It is our deepest fear that we are powerful beyond measure". We have the power to change our world if we dare to believe that we do.

Please choose your values wisely. Deeply feel what is right for your greater self. Believe in them and live by them. By doing so you are exercising your power to change the world.

Every single action makes a difference.

Chapter 12

THE CONSCIOUS LEADER

In chapter two I described consciousness as going hand in hand with awareness and how humans have a unique gift to experience themselves, a gift that other animals do not seem to have. It is my opinion that true consciousness is only experienced when an individual is aware of who they truly are and exactly what their purpose is.

Awareness is not consciousness until it is coupled with purpose.

All living things have awareness. The single cell amoeba has awareness and reacts to its environment. Awareness is a characteristic of life. Animals have awareness of their surroundings and react accordingly. A rabbit can sense danger from a distance and a dog can sense fear in another animal. Some plants react to the sun by opening and shutting their flowers to maximise energy intake and to attract, and even catch, insects. The distinction with humans is that we have the potential to experience the awareness of our own being. Of course that can be a curse when the experience is derived from the fear-based ego. In that context, self-awareness is not necessarily related to consciousness. A human being becomes truly conscious when they can experience and know themselves and know their purpose. That is, they know why they exist beyond the ego and accept that they are a part of something much greater. That is true consciousness.

None of us can experience a truly conscious existence until we know where and why we fit in. Without purpose we are marginally removed from other animals and our only claim to fame that we sit at the top of the food chain. We are the shark of the ocean or the lion of the jungle. This is what we are experiencing on planet earth at the moment. An environment dominated by an intelligent life form (and I use that term fairly generously) without a predator, except other humans themselves. An intelligent life form without competition that is able to consume when and what it chooses. That is not conscious living and until we have developed a sense of our greater purpose we are simply consumers with an elevated degree of awareness. Just like the bacteria in the dish, happily exploiting our environment, oblivious to the consequences of our extravagance and ignorance.

Having a sense of our purpose puts us in a position where we are no longer just consumers but conscious creators - beings that understand where they fit and their responsibility to maintain a healthy organism (body and earth). Surely that is no more than we would expect of our own cells. We are then like healthy cells in a healthy body and no longer a virus, rather immune system cells capable of healing the greater organism we know as earth.

Science has shown us that each living cell in the body has its own intelligence and awareness to react to its environment. Our body is basically a community of these individual cells living in harmony for the betterment of the entire being. In relation to earth, it is the human race that represents the community of smaller parts with its own intelligence (earth cells) that has the responsibility to harmonise for the betterment of the entire planet. In our own bodies, the individual cells each play their part. Planet earth is no different. We alone have the capacity to either destroy our own species, along with many other species, or contribute to a happy, healthy earth. Earth will eventually heal itself. It is simply a matter of whether we wish to remain a part of our host or not. We have the potential to bring consciousness to the life of our planet. I for one really enjoy life and know it would be a great pity if we were unable to arrest our current unconscious slide into oblivion. I believe we can, and will, together. I see evidence of our expanding consciousness every day. You have chosen this book and made it to chapter twelve for goodness sake!

I would like to expand on this comparison between our own bodies and planet earth. On earth, humans represent the thinking intelligent part of the organism, a bit like the brain and nervous system in our own bodies. We have the ability to be consciously aware and influence creation in the best interests of our host. Collectively we produce the thinking for earth and those thoughts collectively create the reality. Currently our thoughts are scattered and few of us create harmoniously. If this were happening inside a human brain the individual would be branded mentally unstable and most likely locked up for his or her own protection. I have absolutely no doubt that an alien life form observing the behaviour of the collective brain cells of planet earth would reach the very same diagnosis. That may explain why aliens only come to earth on such short visits? They think it is a loony bin!

I believe that our true purpose is to consciously, and together, enrich the health of our planet and ourselves, and enjoy the learning experience of doing so.

Yes, it is also about fun. No one said that living had to be difficult. We just make it that way with our fearful thoughts. Have you ever seen a worried bird or a stressed out fish in the wild? The highly conscious leader values the importance of fun and being light, regardless of the perceived seriousness of the situation. I mean to say, if death is not serious then what is? This does not mean they will not at times feel fear from old conditioning and beliefs. The difference is, they will still take conscious action *despite* that fear. That is the true definition of courage. Courage is not the lack of fear but the ability to act, despite the existence of fear. Highly conscious individuals understand it is a privilege to experience life on planet earth and they are grateful for the opportunity for that experience and all it brings. They have the ability to influence others through their own behaviours and actions. They influence by what they do. They appreciate we are all in effect leaders and work with others for the best outcomes for all. They understand the meaning of win-win.

Leadership is not a position it is a way of being. It is not what an individual does for a living or has written on their business card. It is not about having money or the perceived power of wealth. Leaders are role models. Conscious leaders have a strong sense of 'true' purpose and understand where they fit in the bigger picture, beyond themselves. They act from their strong sense of 'true' purpose and are no more than that. Above all, conscious leaders are not perfect. They are still learning.

The highly conscious leader will choose, create or support a business that has a clear and visible purpose that supports sustainable outcomes for our planet and all of its inhabitants.

How could they do anything less? They care about themselves and appreciate that they are more than just their body and mind. Their chosen business could be any industry at all. It could be the oil industry. Bear with me here. The visible purpose that supports sustainable outcomes for our planet and all inhabitants, in the case of the oil industry, would be to remediate the damage already done by oil production and effectively transition to other sustainable energy sources, with urgency. After all, petrol cars will not disappear overnight. The highly conscious leader will understand this while appreciating the necessity to let go of old fearful ways and enthusiastically pursue alternate energy models. They will work collaboratively with other industries on transition strategies. They will appreciate that the industry itself is bound by the laws of nature and is reaching (more likely passed) the end of its life cycle, as every other living organism does. They will understand and accept that change is a constant and that oil has had its day in the sun. They know that the oil industry, as a part of all connected life, must eventually die and that death is only a transition of the energetic matter back into the universal energy pool. The transitioned energy will be available to create an energy model that supports all life on planet earth.

They understand that to resist natural cycles is unhealthy for life itself. They understand that they can, and do, make a difference.

The highly conscious leader understands the connectivity of all things and considers holistic solutions. They understand that the best decisions will be made from the heart, not the head. They will have the ability to control the mind and use thought effectively, but sparingly. Instead of reacting they will consciously choose.

Thinking is practical in solving problems. Feeling is fundamental in making holistic decisions.

The highly conscious leader understands that the ego is controlled by fear. They use the full power of their whole heart and mind to support their vision. They understand and accept the universal truth that all things are connected and, therefore, equally valued. They relish their life journey with passion. They love being alive while, at the same time, appreciate death is simply a part of the life cycle. They are grateful for the opportunity to tread this earth. They understand fear and its relationship to the workings of the ego. They engage and work collaboratively with people of similar values and beliefs and understand the best outcomes come from working with others. They appreciate that conflict is not only unnecessary, but also unproductive. They accept that others will have differing views on reality and value their input. They have balance in their life. They are not what they do; they are what they believe in and how they do it. While passion is evident in all aspects of their life, the work they do simply compliments who they really are, and what they stand for. They do not judge others while understanding that they may be required to make decisions involving judgement. They understand their own purpose and live in alignment with it.

Conscious leaders appreciate that life is a learning experience and that they are just as much a student as a teacher.

They are consistent because they are real and authentic. A highly conscious individual will act from a state of heightened awareness based on feelings from the heart, rather than thoughts from the head, in all aspects of their life. They take a holistic view on the world. They spend as much time in the present moment as possible, understanding that any feelings that are not of a loving nature are coming from outside the present moment. They understand how their ego works and exercise control by relinquishing the need to have control. They can make tough decisions knowing the decision was made in the best interests of the whole, and accept that may not be immediately apparent to some.

They will really 'see you'. Anyone that has seen the movie Avatar will remember the use of this phrase in the movie. The story is set on a far away planet paradise, being plundered by humans for its resources in the name of profit. Does anyone see any similarity to what is happening right now in our own paradise? The peaceful alien inhabitants of this spiritual planet (Indigenous tribes) use the term 'I see you' as an indication of deep love. It refers to seeing as not with the eyes, but with a total and holistic understanding and respect of the other person. A feeling and deep appreciation of who the other really is, and true acceptance of the connection between them, and the value they represent. That is how a truly conscious leader will see another. This is in effect seeing beyond the perception of the mind, looking beyond the reflection of light that the eyes interpret as a human being, and really connecting with the true beauty of the glorious consciousness before them. This is seeing without the influence of the ego, in effect sensing the energy field of another living being. This is truly an 'in the moment' experience of the other and represents an ability to access a state of pure unconditional love for another being. Unconditional love has no judgement.

While this sets quite a high bar, I also understand that life beyond the perception of ego is not a sacrifice, rather something to be cherished. Happiness and contentment reside in the present moment where the ego is still. True happiness exists in the now where fearful thoughts are absent. We achieve this state when we gaze at a beautiful sunrise or when a mother looks at her newborn baby. That look beyond what our eyes think they see. It is more of a feeling thing than a seeing thing. That is how we will view each other when we are all living consciously and have genuine respect for all life.

If you look behind the greedy behaviours currently demonstrated by leaders all around us, in the search for offensive levels of wealth and power, it is easy to blame money for being the source of all evil. Money in itself is not evil, however the greed for money is certainly not a conscious pursuit. Why do we have this obsession with money? If you look beyond the bank balance, the reason we pursue money is because of the feeling that having money gives us. This could be a feeling of security, or freedom to do what we want, or just feeling safe. The question I would ask is - why do we have this obsession of accumulating money and wealth, driving our absurd behaviours on this planet, when all we are really after is a feeling? Why is that so? If we can find another way to get these feelings, do we need money at all? If we can feel safe and free without money then surely there is no need for our obsessive pursuit of it?

Money is simply a currency of love. It is used to represent that which is given and received. The paper itself has no true value. If you have any doubts about that, do some research on the collateral supposedly backing the currency markets? Its only real value is the feelings it can bring to you. A conscious leader understands that money is not evil, nor is it the primary objective for happiness. The feelings we seek are available through a number of ways other than money. A conscious leader will understand that our feelings arise from our thoughts and we can change the way we feel by changing the way we think.

Does the accumulation of more money make your feelings of security and freedom any stronger? We have already established that our feelings come from our thoughts and beliefs. Consequently, the need for large wads of money is only a reflection of a fear based subconscious belief. If it is challenging you to accumulate the amount of money you want then change your perception and get the feeling you want, without the money. Dream you are safe and free. Imagine you can do what you want. Remember life is only a perception of our thoughts, skewed from very limited data and processed through an unreliable filter that we barely understand. Believe you have what you want and guess what? You have what you want because you feel you have what you want, and isn't that what you are after in the first place, to feel the way you want to feel?

Material possessions are only a temporary means to satisfy our desire and need to have a feeling. People with few material possessions, living in poverty, can still feel happy, and more often than not they do. Conversely, there are many cases of depression and suicide involving people who are extremely wealthy. I was relatively wealthy when I had my emotional breakdown. The main reason this happens is the constant fear of losing the material things that are supposed to make us happy in the first place. Happiness is internal. Happiness resides within us and is achieved by being present and having clear and positive thoughts about our environment and ourselves. Material possessions can be taken away or lost. Inner peace and self-love can never be taken away. It is a part of who you are. Conscious leaders know this.

Thought is useful in solving problems. Humans possess an amazing gift, by way of their thinking minds. When used consciously, and not distorted by fear, the mind can achieve incredible outcomes. That red Porsche can really do some amazing stuff when in the hands of a competent driver. On the other hand, feeling is basic to making the best holistic decisions and to achieving true happiness. The heart must be consulted. Feelings and emotions are valuable guides and more in tune with our intuition than thought. Our intuition is our sense of connection to the universal intelligence, or the pool of all knowledge. That's right, even more than Google itself!

Intuition is like hindsight in advance.

We do not access true joy through thinking. True joy is a way of being that can only be experienced by the feeling of being connected with our true self.

Chapter 13

THE CONSCIOUS BUSINESS

So how will the highly conscious business look and feel?

A conscious business will have a clear purpose aligned to restoring and nurturing our planet and all living things on it. I call this conscious customer service. This will be the driving force and passion of the board, the executive and the staff. The emphasis of every single policy and practice will be on sustainable outcomes that feel right.

While profit will not drive behaviour the making of a profit is a sustainable outcome.

A business must still deliver a profit. Making money is not a bad thing. All thriving life forms produce excess energy. There are bills to be paid. The ongoing viability of any enterprise relies on having and attracting sufficient capital to continue developing better practice, and reaching more sustainable objectives. All living things should make a positive difference to life, and for business a profit can be a positive contribution. A truly values driven business understands that any money they make is simply received in exchange for the conscious service and love that they have given to others. However, unlike corporate giants today, the value of the company will not be measured by the amount of money that they make, share price or market capitalisation. The value of the business will be measured against the success in delivering on its purpose. That is what the annual report will focus on. That is why staff will be engaged and passionate about their work and that is why customers will use its services and buy its products.

There will be absolute transparency. Everyone will know the true purpose of the business and why it exists. That means complete disclosure about its actions, ownership structure and financial performance. No secrets. No need. No conflicts of interest because all involved have a common interest. The purpose will drive the behaviour. A conscious business has a highly visible purpose and a focus on meeting its purpose aligned objectives.

A purpose driven business is typified by the conscious decision making of passionate people focussed on achieving exceptional and sustainable outcomes for the planet and its inhabitants through the delivery of consciously created products and conscious caring service.

Imagine for a moment the boardroom of an enlightened and highly conscious business? The atmosphere in the boardroom will be cooperative, light and friendly. Directors will be passionate and caring people, not necessarily business heavyweights. The gender mix will be naturally balanced, as will the life experience and cultural diversity. When I refer to gender mix I am referring to women in a true feminine sense. Women that contribute at a heart level, not necessarily high powered business women that have engaged their masculinity to survive, as is currently the case in the corporate boys' club. Rather than some archaic affirmative action legislation driving female participation, a sustainable enterprise, in a sustainable environment, will value a balance of female energy to fulfil its true purpose. Lets face it, men have not done all that well so far. The feminine represents the mother. The mother is associated with nurturing and protecting and that sits nicely with a purpose of restoring and nurturing our planet.

A conscious business will be a learning organisation. Just like us, business will cast a reflection. There are always opportunities for doing things better and better outcomes come from the collective ideas of many. The business will value the self-development of its people, and their opinions. The business will want better outcomes for its customers. They will achieve this by investing in ways of engaging customers and listening to their suggestions. Both of these activities help build a relevant and performance driven culture. Remember, performance is measured by results against purpose not just profit!

A positive and heart based board, or owners, will inspire heartfelt and conscious leaders wanting to be a part of something that is making a positive difference in the world. They are engaged with the vision and purpose of the company. The organisation will have values that drive the way it does business and treats its consumers and suppliers. The key measure of staff performance will be the way that they go about their work. Outcomes will be measured against the true purpose, not so much on financial returns, although financial returns will be considered valuable.

I had a similar vision when I was a senior executive with an Australian Credit Union. The concept of a credit union is quite appealing. Credit unions have a mutual status; they are owned by the membership. The membership is comprised of the staff and the customers. These members held all of the shares. There are no financial returns to be made from being a shareholder. A shareholder is a member that can vote to elect a Board. Any profits generated from operations are normally returned to the business for the benefit of the members through the delivery of better services and products. In this particular credit union, only active customers can be members. That is they have to physically have an account. The actual product offering is very similar to banks with the exception that the profits from sales are not distributed to shareholders. The purpose of the credit union is to provide efficient services and support to local communities. The original concept delivered a more locally owned and operated financial services model offering personalised service, and keeping profits in the local region. Operate locally, employ locally, spend locally and invest locally. The market requirement for a degree of operating scale has lead to different credit unions working cooperatively to compete with larger banks in the wider market, without losing their local identity.

The integrity of that noble model has been somewhat lost due to the creation of much larger nationally operating mutual models, often capable of behaving very much like the big banks. Regardless, the concept is still a good one. The credit union that I was involved with had developed an amazing culture among its staff. There were open lines of communication between front line staff, executives and members. The focus was on the member with a passion about being authentic, and just a little bit cheeky. I recall a strategic planning session where the executive team likened the business model to a hotted up Kombi, as opposed to the BMW banks! We saw our business as a cheeky upstart punching well above its weight. The unique selling proposition (USP) was an ethical one. The business differentiated its purpose from the banks by promoting the notion that customers had the choice to bank locally, where profits went back to members through local investment, or use a corporate bank where profits were paid out to institutional investors in Sydney or overseas. It was, and still is, a powerful point of difference.

The member engagement scores were amazing. During the strategic review process, a group of external analysts, engaged to measure customer loyalty, unearthed an engagement score for staff and members, higher than they had ever seen in the finance industry, by a considerable margin. Sick leave absences were negligible. The business cared for the people and the people cared for the business. It was a great place to work.

An example of the culture was typified in the "Well Day" policy. This policy allowed staff to schedule a day off from their sick leave entitlement to simply have fun or do something health enriching, such as spending time with their family. No need to take a sickie, take a wellie! Other paid days leave were available for attending community events with family along with generous self-development leave to study. Teams had access to staff wellness programs that included massage and meditation therapy, in the workplace. The place was humming. Customers remained loyal; notwithstanding they were often being charged slightly higher lending margins than the banks, and despite attractive offers from larger competitors to move their business. Staff were not focussed on remuneration and remained happily employed, despite the level of wages being less than that of larger banks. You just can't buy that. The financial performance reflected the internal health of the people. Annual growth rates were well in excess of the industry.

Unfortunately, a change of leadership has seen that priceless culture pretty much destroyed overnight. The incumbent Chief Executive retired and his replacement was recruited from a public service accounting background and had neither, a concept of heart matters, nor any appreciation of the value of relationships. Not a great mix in a relationship business in a relational universe. The Chief Executive was high on academic intelligence but low on feeling and consciousness. Many of the aforesaid staff policies were removed and leadership morphed to management by fear. Decision-making became secretive and hidden agendas and rumour thrived. Open communication was stifled and staff engagement tumbled. Large numbers of the passionate and loyal workforce moved on and, within a very short period, the dynamic culture that had taken decades to develop was lost forever. Interestingly, the focus on purely financial indicators actually diminished the financial performance of the business. The business lost sight of its true purpose of being ... its members. The workplace is now a toxic environment enveloped in fear and misinformation.

It is my view that people will engage both as clients and employees when they see a clear purpose and understand how their involvement will contribute to that purpose. They want to feel a part of something bigger. That is the blueprint of the highly conscious business model. People want to work there because they can see that they are making a difference. Customers want to do business there because they can see that they are supporting a honourable purpose. I have absolutely no doubt that people genuinely do care provided they feel they can make a difference. There is that feeling word again. It is a feeling, not a thinking thing. Ultimately it is all about being authentic, being passionate and being real.

A highly conscious business will not require fancy marketing or advertising campaigns to attract clients. It will attract customers by doing exactly what it says it will do, acting responsibly and caring. After all it is about *what you do*, not what you say you do. People will feel the difference. The Law of Attraction works even more dynamically with conscious groups than it does with individuals.

————

I am currently mentoring a young financial planner who is in the process of establishing a highly ethical business model of her own. Rachael has become disenchanted with the financial advice industry, due to some less than transparent commission practices. The industry is ranked poorly in the trust stakes. A 2014 Roy Morgan - Ethics and Honesty Poll ranked financial planners well below bank managers and lawyers, and only marginally above television reporters and journalists. The poor old used car salesperson remains in the least trusted occupation, while nurses scored a massive 325% above planners! Not surprisingly, politicians, business executives and union leaders ranked very poorly. It seems that we are aware of the lack of consciousness in this group but not sure how to change it. More precisely, we do not yet believe in our own power to change it.

Rachael's vision is to have total transparency in product and pricing and she has a clear purpose. She wants to educate her clients to achieve the best individual outcomes for them, while creating value for her local community through a profit distribution model to selected charities. It is really exciting to work with her on such a principled venture. It restores my faith in humanity and represents a working example of what can be done. Business can lead the change, although it seems that any major change in large business consciousness will need to be driven from the bottom up, and that is of course by us as consumers.

I would also like to share another personal experience involving a local not for profit disabilities service, of which I am currently the chairperson. I had never had any previous exposure to the disabilities sector before joining this board. The General Manager of R&R Disabilities originally contracted me to do some work on the employee Enterprise Agreement late in 2011. The disabilities industry is undergoing a period of great uncertainty as the funding model changes from the direct funding of service organisations to handing the control of funding to the clients. The change is designed to empower families with disabilities, enabling them to choose a service that best meets their needs. A truly sensible aim, I think you would agree. The proposal potentially threatened the cash flow of the service as it's revenue was no longer guaranteed by government and would be subject to the demands of its users. Of course, through my finance background, I was very familiar with this as a standard business-operating model. When I was asked to help on the board, I felt I could make a difference. My first meeting was the Annual General Meeting, where I expected to be nominated to the board. I left the meeting ten minutes later as the chairperson. Set up? Absolutely! Regrets? None whatsoever.

The first couple of years have been about bolstering the skill set and makeup of the board, agreeing a longer-term strategy, understanding our costs and getting the financial reporting simplified. The aim was to get simple graphs and financial pictures that summarise the business performance allowing all board members, and staff, to easily understand the financial picture without the need of an accounting degree. The board now has a composition of broad skills including corporate business, industry, self-development, carers, sales, marketing, finance and human resources. The most important consideration was to have families, and carers of people with disabilities, strongly represented at board level. Our purpose is to provide development and growth opportunities to those with a disability and we never want to lose sight of why we exist.

This is a truly heart based organisation and the board and staff are totally committed to the purpose of "Enabling Fuller Life Experiences". It is all about the clients and their families. Once the financial picture was stable and understood the focus returned to why we exist. The board papers are divided into the following categories in order of our priority;

1. Our Clients
2. Our People

3. Financial
4. Risk and Compliance
5. Other

Our purpose, or reason for being, is our clients and they must be our first consideration. If we are not giving this group priority are we still relevant? Of course we need to have the best and most passionate staff and volunteers, including board members, to deliver our promise to our clients. My view has always been that if you get these first two factors right then the financial performance will pretty well take care of itself. You can see that this represents a totally opposite view to the Chief Executive in my credit union story. I can confirm that the financial growth of this organisation is outstanding and revenues have risen at around thirty percent per annum. Of course prudent management of finances, compliance and safety is a key risk that has to be managed, but a conscious business must never lose sight of its purpose and this order of priority keeps R&R clearly focused on its purpose.

Should the enterprise ever consider a merger or partnership, the same order of importance would guide our deliberations. What benefit does it bring to our clients? What benefit does it bring to our people and so on? If there was a substantial financial advantage to be gained from a merger or acquisition that we believed had a diluting, or adverse, impact on our clients or staff, the answer would be a simple no. It is an unpretentious, but effective philosophy that keeps the business focussed on purpose.

The true significance of this service is no more typified than at the annual families' Christmas party. I recall my awkwardness when inviting some local dignitaries and trying to describe the event. I asked the Mayor of Coffs Harbour had she ever been to a party where the invitees were required to throw down six tequila slammers before entering, and how that party looked thirty minutes later? I should point out that the Mayor did not have any personal experience with this sort of party, which made me think that my youth may have been slightly misspent. Regardless of that glaring disparity in our upbringing, I went on to explain to her that this was the best comparison I could give about the R&R Christmas party, with the exception that there is *no alcohol*. As soon as the music starts the dance floor is swamped with joyous happy and beautiful souls, smiling and having a ball, totally uninhibited, wheel chairs and all. It does not stop until the party is finished. What a wonderful experience and one that reminds us all why we actually do what we do! R&R employees give of their own time to be cooks, washers and attendants on the night. From my observations, they have just as much fun as anyone else!

I have contemplated my involvement at R&R and can truly say I can never repay what I have received personally from just being involved. That includes the joy of being around passionate and caring people but also feeling safe to open my own heart. I have come to the view that it is the rest of society, us so-called normal humans with our constantly thinking minds and unconscious fears, that have the real disability. It is as if the intellectual disability affecting some of our clients gives them permission to be free, happy and open with their emotions. They are certainly authentic in every possible way. I appreciate there are practical challenges faced by the families but I also appreciate why they make the sacrifices that they do. It is worth every moment.

To be involved with a conscious business, with heart-based purpose, not only makes a difference in the world, it makes a difference in you. There is nothing more special about the people at R&R than at a lot of other organisations. The difference is they are sharing something that is special. Each and every board and staff member is a leader. Each has the power to make a difference, and each does.

When it is all said and done it is up to us as individuals to decide what a business will be. We have the choice to support a business, understand the purpose and choose to engage or not. If, for example, we all stopped buying at Woolworths owned enterprises, because of a hypothetical ethical issue, then they would have to change. They would not have a business if they did not. Each of us has the power of choice. None of us are victims. We just need to be conscious in our choices and remember who we truly are and respect that 'we are powerful beyond measure'.

The growth of social media has really turned business ethics on its head. In the past, in the event of some ethical disaster by a corporate, such as Woolworths, a smooth well fashioned media spokesperson would be rolled out in front of the cameras, and unsurprisingly afforded prime time coverage by the very same media that benefits from the absurd marketing dollars spent by the company at their station. That would be it. The issue would quickly go away. Well not anymore. If there is injustice then we have the ability to source more independent information and publicise our issue via social media. Of course individual views will be coloured by filters, until such time as we can see beyond the perception to which they tie us. The more information we have access to the better our own choices will be.

It is my personal view that we will witness the accelerating destabilisation of the power of multinational corporations over the next decade or so. As we raise our consciousness as consumers, ask more important questions and have access to even more information, we will be inclined to have an even more local focus. Technology has greatly reduced the cost for business to set up remotely and access clients at great distance. The Internet has changed the world forever. Big used to mean powerful but that paradigm is losing significance now when small players can set up small enterprises from home and get more media attention via social media, than those corporates we have developed such a healthy mistrust for. Additionally, our trust and familiarity with local producers and retailers will influence our buying habits. Authentic values aligned to meaningful purpose are attractive to us. We are ready for change. I can feel it.

Consumers really always have had the power; they just did not believe it. Right now that concept is becoming a reality. Change is driven through great leadership. That is, leaders and individuals with vision, principle and purpose all behaving consciously.

That is us.

Chapter 14

THE CONSCIOUS GOVERNMENT

A highly conscious government will have a clearly stated vision for a country or state completely in alignment with, and supportive of, achieving the best possible sustainable outcomes for our planet and all of its inhabitants. The vision will be for a better world for all inhabitants.

Government is a big business. Aside from a number of critical services that it delivers to the public, government has the same responsibilities to operate sustainably in both a financial and environmental sense, as does any other business. This means that government must also be financially sound. While revenue is primarily derived from business and citizens, the books still have to balance. It has to be a sustainable operation in all aspects of that meaning. To print additional currency to stimulate growth, as the United States and other economies have repeatedly allowed, has absolutely no relationship with sustainability at all. Remember the notion of equal forces and unintended consequence from chapter ten? Well these sorts of practices result in widespread hidden consequences in other areas of our connected economies. You can count on that.

Government has a wider obligation to implement policies that both support and encourage the right corporate and individual behaviours, and are responsible in terms of global health. Government represents the public caretaker of the earth and protector of the vulnerable; certainly not a play thing of the rich and powerful. The chest beating, fear fuelled election campaigns, funded by our biggest polluters, do not fool anyone with an ounce of consciousness. It has never been about what politicians say they will do; it is all about what they really stand for and who they really are that matters. In other words, what is their purpose and values?

There is no need for pork barrelling or fear based campaigning in a conscious democracy. The emphasis is on the politician's passion to achieve the vision, and fulfil the purpose of government. Like any business, the government must have a clear vision and values. A government is purely an assembly of people connected by the same universal energy, working towards a vision and common goals. The pursuit of a meaningful vision will require a parliament characterised by compassionate legislation and passionate politicians. Government should be focussed on achieving exceptional and sustainable outcomes for the planet and its inhabitants, through the delivery of consciously crafted policies and caring service. The Public Service should be renamed the Compassionate Service because that is its purpose, the delivery of services to the most vulnerable with heart felt compassion. This includes the police force, defence force, nurses, teachers and taxation personnel, all of whom will have a passion to truly deliver on the mission and purpose of the government in the most efficient and caring way. Before you burst into raucous laughter, why not? If we can imagine this happening then it surely can happen. The only limiting factor, for what is possible, is our own imagination. Until we can actually see and feel this happening there is little hope of it ever eventuating, so please give it consideration. It might seem like a far off dream right now but we simply have to change.

The purpose of government is not something that is decided by a particular party at election time. The purpose is a constant and meaningful vision for the future, not a slogan. The strategy for a nation or municipality does not belong to a political party. It belongs to the nation or community. It is not a fluctuating fantasy but rather a solid and compassionate purpose that considers the connectedness of all things.

In essence, a highly conscious government will be made up of highly conscious people. And just how is that going to happen? The world will have highly conscious consumers and voters. This is where you and I come in. People have the power and we must not be afraid to use it. Our power lies in our conscious awareness to exercise choice and ask questions. The current party system cannot exist in a conscious world where there would be no need for an opposition because we have elected honest, transparent and passionate leaders, focused on delivering the vision of the government and nothing more. WE have the power to make that happen. It is time we owned that power.

As voters and consumers we must remember, "Our deepest fear is not that we are inadequate. Our deepest fear is that we are powerful beyond measure". We do hold the power.

There is no current model of effective government and, like so many others, I have become increasingly disillusioned and frustrated with the behaviour and performance of our political decision makers. The way things are currently structured a change of government will not change any of that. The system is flawed and encourages short term self interest over long-term visionary action. The electoral system is flawed and complex. A conscious government would fix that as a matter of priority. The entire fabric of government, including policies and process, must be totally transparent. The current preferences system, operating in Australia, works like a chook raffle. Even the candidates have little idea how the preferences will impact their vote. We all have a responsibility to fix this ridiculous state of affairs, as soon as possible.

Party politics, as I alluded, is flawed. It is toxic. The evidence is clear. The system continually delivers us egocentric show people that put self-preservation and self-interest ahead of the long-term wellbeing of all stakeholders. They habitually pander to elite factions that exert control through lobby groups, opinion polls and financiers. We need a parliament of independently thinking and caring people. That is how it must be. We do not need party politics. The day of a party giving us limited options is old paradigm thinking. The people will decide on the priorities from a position of conscious deliberation and in the broader interests of our earth. Once a strategic vision, defining a countries role in the global healing, has been agreed, it is then up to the elected representatives to work on achieving the goals and delivering on the strategy. It is utter lunacy to change strategy and vision every time there is an election. The key components of conscious government will be;

1) Responsible fiscal management (balanced financials)
2) Coordinated services to the most vulnerable
3) Education and Wellness
4) Emergency and security services
5) Global responsibility

The whole structure of the education system is also flawed. The current rigid structure should be dismantled and replaced with a program that teaches children to learn, to understand their egos and how they work, and informs them about universal laws and responsible stewardship of our planet. The old thinking that defines success as a six-figure salary and a fancy title on a business card would be replaced with the vision of achieving a life purpose and being happy and healthy.

The curriculum should be designed to enable children to learn about who they truly are and what conscious creation actually is. It will show them how their thoughts create true happiness and enrich their planet, how wellbeing is simply in the way that they think, and that fear is an illusion. This is what our children need to learn. They need to appreciate the power of their own light and how love sustains life. Once our kids get this they can learn anything. It's all on the net for goodness sake! It is common knowledge that it is much easier to teach skills than it is to change behaviours. Develop the beliefs and values of our youth as a priority and then teach them skills and competencies when they have chosen their career purpose. Teach them that beliefs should be held lightly.

Children develop their filters and beliefs in the first seven years of life. We have a responsibility to teach them about their own power and about love and not fear.

———

Government is not a political game it is a very big business. It must be lead and managed like any business and by the best possibly qualified people. By qualified I do not necessarily mean academics. Specialist academic advice can, and should be, consulted as part of any decision making process. By best qualified I mean truly inspired, compassionate, honest, impassioned, transparent and loving people, not afraid of leading and taking hard decisions and who embrace a holistic approach to the business of governing, and its part in supporting the world in which we live. Real people that care and feel. Authentic and caring individuals, not perfect but conscious.

The current democratic system, comprising established parties offering limited choice, is at the mercy of the swinging vote, estimated at around a quarter of eligible adult voters in any electorate. This would indicate that the great majority of us have beliefs that are so entrenched we will not change our vote regardless of the performance of our party of choice. That is very scary indeed! Important stakeholders, such as our planet, are not even considered. The grossly rich and powerful really call the shots, a situation we have allowed to develop through our own apathy and disbelief in our own power.

At the time of writing this book the incumbent government in Australia is about to table legislation that would enshrine vaccinations as compulsory for those on welfare payments. Recipients would lose their support pensions if they do not conform and have their children immunised. The legislation takes away choice from the most vulnerable families. Who stands to benefit from this policy financially? Multi National drug companies that is who! This antiquated piece of regulation totally excludes the leanings of quantum physics and other proven research that informs us our cells respond to our environment. Disease is just a symptom. Restore a healthy and loving environment and disease will not survive. Our bodies have natural defence mechanisms in place, perfectly capable of maintaining life, if not overridden by fearful thoughts and poisoned by our own greedy behaviours. This is a perfect example of fearful law making. How could this still be happening in such a vibrant and well-educated country as Australia, with all we now know? There is so much to be done.

Current political direction fluctuates at the whim of opinion polls that are sensationally promoted through the media to support their own business models. A conscious government would not react on the impulse of opinion polls. Leading is never about popularity. Leading is about setting an example and doing what is right and in alignment with purpose.

In quantum terms, the only stakeholder to any business or government is the earth. It just has to be. We are of the earth and intrinsically connected. Governments are only a representation of people and people are part of the greater organism we call earth. The vision of a conscious government would embody this connection and deliver policies that support all life, not just human life.

A typical example of this obsession with human life above all other life occurred only recently in the small community of Bellingen near my home town. The dispute involved a colony of fruit bats. Humans, as we have already discussed, have historically invaded the habitat of all living creatures with scant regard for the consequences. The fruit bat now has limited places to breed and feed these days and, as an unintended consequence, can impact on our space from time to time. They eat from our fruit tress. They have to because we destroyed their natural food supply. Bats are also noisy and can spread disease, but hey so do humans. Have you been to a rave party lately and how did you catch your last cold? There has been a tussle between local and state government as to who has the authority to deal with the unruly colonies of bats that have raised the ire of some local residents. Yes just some, not even a majority.

Eventually the state government handed control back to the council on the condition that - "whatever action was taken, human health would not be compromised'. In effect that means you can do what you damn well like as long as humans are not disturbed. This attitude of humans above all other forms of life is not in alignment with conscious government. Our earth is represented by all of the living creatures that make up our ecosystem. Humans have a responsibility, and dare I say purpose, to contribute consciously toward the prosperity of the planet. It is important to note that prosperity is not about bank balance and wealth; it must encompass the health and well being of all life. Our earth, and you and I as a part of our earth, deserve that.

I was recently driving past the Bongil Bongil National Park, between Urunga and Coffs Harbour to the north, and admiring the natural beauty of those old forest trees and plants. The birds were in full voice and the world seemed at peace. I felt so grateful that the state had locked up that beautiful area for nature and the limited recreation of man. That particular area of the park is around forty square kilometres, which seems substantial when one man is standing alone in the forest.

The reality is quite different when one considers the original forest coverage of our planet before industrialisation, only a few hundred years ago. Just as two hundred years is a nano second in the evolution of life on earth, so to is forty square kilometres just a speck in comparison to the original volume of forest in existence before man realised there was money in timber. We congratulate ourselves for preserving such small areas of beauty when in reality it is just a token gesture.

The world is past the stage of making what we have sustainable. We clearly have an obligation to restore the health of our environment. Our planet is sick. The current situation, with regard to water and air quality and land degradation, will never sustain our ongoing wellbeing. We are simply surviving.

We are past sustainable practice: we are clearly in restoration mode.

Obviously, our rate of population growth is not sustainable. I cringe when I hear developers say that the earth could sustain much more human life if we genetically modify our food and opened up more land for development. What about the rest of life? We are already well beyond what our planet can reasonably share with nature. We are out of balance. Once again this is a symptom of an unconscious species. As we raise the consciousness of the planet, through expanding human consciousness, population will naturally adjust to sustainable levels. We will know.

I recently saw a documentary on television; yes I do succumb to television despite some of the disparaging statements I may make about the media, I just try to avoid the rubbish. Thank goodness for remotes! Anyway, in this program some scientists were researching the environmental damage that humans have caused to the earth over the past three hundred years or so. That is less than a blink of an eye in the four and a half billion-year timespan of earth. Less than a drop in the Pacific Ocean, yet the damage is monumental. The show graphically simulated what they believed would be the outcome if insects became extinct. Plants would not be germinated, birds would die and the whole ecosystem would collapse. Weather patterns would be affected and earth would become a desolate dust bowl within a short time. They then ran a model of life on earth if the human race became extinct. Over time all of the damage we have caused would be repaired. Plants would return to where we had once cleared. Birds and animals would flourish in perfect balance, and the natural forces of nature would erode our buildings. Our seas would return to rich oceans of life and our climate would become more stable. It was quite confronting to be honest. I felt ashamed to know that I was partly responsible. The earth would be so much better off without us! I should point out that those simulations presumed that people would continue to live unconsciously. As conscious beings we have the power to heal our planet and enjoy wonderful lives, but don't for a minute believe that our earth would miss us one little bit if we continue behaving the way we do now.

I have some empathy with those that believe in a global government. There is no doubt that we have to start thinking globally, and not just economically, to account for our total connectedness. There will always be cultural differences across the planet and a need for more local delivery of services, which necessitates a structure with appropriate localised autonomy. However, an overarching framework to coordinate and share best practice, technology and abundance makes perfect sense to me. The notion of having our environment divided up into individual countries, all competing against each other at some level and yet all surviving only because of our shared planet, makes absolutely no sense at all. When the hundredth monkey becomes conscious we will shake our heads in disbelief at what we have created. I am sure a lot of you are already shaking your heads.

Governments must take responsibility for the patch of earth that they administer, while simultaneously considering the impact on the whole planet. Bats, fish and kangaroos do not get to vote, nor do they have the ability to act consciously. The human race has a responsibility to live consciously on behalf of all living things. We are the brain and heart of our fragile planet. It is time we took responsibility.

One global policy that is desperately needed is applying 'true cost' methodology to everything that we buy or manufacture. What is the 'true cost' of a product or service after all global impacts are taken into account?

The "true cost" is the real cost when all considerations, including the cost to ensure that there is absolutely no adverse impact on our environment during the entire life cycle of the product or service, are factored into the price. The cost then reflects the whole investment required to restore the environment to its original condition, as existed before the product was made. Lets take the supermarket cost of a bottle of a popular soft drink. The shelf price for a litre of Coke is generally around two dollars. At that price the product generates a profit for the manufacturer, the transporter, the wholesaler and the retailer. If we look at the "true cost" of the product we would need to consider such things as;

- the environmental cost of mining the minerals to make the plastic bottle
- the environmental cost of emissions from the manufacturing plant that moulds the bottle
- the power required during manufacture and the cost to the environment of producing and transporting that power to the factory
- the environmental cost of producing the ingredients, particularly the sugar, from farming practices
- the emissions from transportation and the mobile sales force
- the production and recycling of any packaging materials

- the recycling cost of the plastic bottle after use
- the medical cost from the known health conditions from consuming soft drink including diabetes, tooth decay and obesity to name a few

Maybe a litre of Coke actually costs our planet **ten dollars!**

You may be able to think of other hidden costs to our earth as well. It makes complete sense to look at all products in this way and establish what is the true cost, or financial and environmental consequences, to our planet. If we are not considering all of these factors in a product we are indisputably creating 'unintended consequences' for humanity. Imagine the true cost of coal and oil! Neither would be affordable, and nor should they be. I would imagine that petrol would be at least ten to fifteen times more expensive at the pump to account for the extensive damage bill that comes from using it. By using a true cost calculation we can start to get a real pricing comparison on each product. That enables us to make an educated choice. I have no doubt that with true cost applied, renewable energy would be so much cheaper than fossil fuel that we would all be driving electric cars and have self sufficient power sources in our homes and businesses within ten years! All we are doing at the moment is distorting the pricing in the market for the benefit of rich and powerful interests. That unsustainable behaviour does not serve us now and will not endure in a conscious world. If we know the true cost of a product or service then we are in a position to make an informed choice as consumers.

True cost is a natural way of measuring real monetary value.

The human race has an exceptional ability to respond to changing conditions and markets. Of course there would have to be a carefully managed transition but we have to start somewhere. We have an amazing way of responding to change. We are made that way. Babies have to learn everything from their environment after birth and we continue learning until we die. This is what can save us. This is change we will create by becoming more conscious of our own choices. The markets will respond. They always do.

I have toyed with the idea of an alternate political model. It is clear that democracy does not work. Our choice is severely limited by party politics and the media deliberately confuses us, or should I say those controlling the media do. Dictatorships are dangerous without a truly conscious leader and communism has its own systemic issues. The best I could come up with was a not for profit structure, with an elected governing board holding responsibility for the character of any candidates endorsed to stand for election. Even then that board would have to be made up of exceptional people and who would decide on the foundational members of that board? I decided this is not a thinking thing and that our elevated state of love and awareness would present the solution when the time is right.

At the end of the day I resolved that the real solution lies in grass roots action. It is all about the cells taking responsibility for the organism. It is about all of us fulfilling our roles and following our own true purpose.

The way will be shown.

Chapter 15

WHAT NOW – WHAT CAN WE DO?

Are you happy with the world as it is? Do you shake your head in disbelief at some of the news on TV? Have you seen enough of war, extremist religion, violence and corruption? I know we can do so much better and I believe there is a way forward. We can save our beautiful planet, and ourselves with it.

I said right at the beginning of this book that, in my view, the cause of the current destructive chaos happening on earth right now is our own low level of consciousness as a race. I believe that the way to raise the consciousness of our planet is for each of us individually to raise our own level of consciousness.

Our earth is a living organism made up of trillions upon trillions of smaller living parts, no different to our own bodies that have trillions of individual living cells, existing in harmony to maintain our life. For all we know those minute parts are made up of many trillions more, yet unknown miniscule parts. Life is one big soup made up of tiny living parts. That soup is a highly conscious and intelligent broth.

Just as we would want for all of the cells in our body to be vibrant and healthy, and fulfil their purpose in affording us a happy, healthy and joyous life, so must we as tiny parts of a bigger living world, do the same.

Our ability to impact our world, and the universe, is no different than the ability of our own living cells to impact our health. If left in a healthy environment our cells will dutifully fulfil their purpose and promote a healthy body. A healthy environment is one with unconditional love and without fear. It is a widely accepted belief that self-love is the most important ingredient in leading a healthy and happy life. Our own level of consciousness and self-love directly affects the performance of our cells and the sub atomic particles that make them up. We determine the environment for our cells through our thoughts and actions. We have influence over our own health. We have the choice to be healthy.

Our world is simply a larger living body and each of us is in effect a living cell in that greater body. Whereas our own consciousness will dictate the health of our own cells, giving us sole responsibility for our own health, so to our consciousness is a contributor to the environment of our larger living body (earth). We can achieve global health through our own combined conscious behaviours. Our world will be a healthy and vibrant life form when we, its living cells, are in alignment with love and not run by fear. When we are awake and living consciously. Living consciously is all about understanding our own purpose, and our part in the health of earth, and living our lives accordingly.

As a part of my own professional consulting activities I run strategic planning sessions for business and one of the favourite lines I use to explain the aim of having and reviewing a strategy and purpose is "When you are up to your arse in alligators it is easy to forget that the original objective was to drain the swamp". This is an interpretation from an old American proverb. Roughly translated this means that when we are so busy stressing about all of the routine stuff in our daily lives, it is easy to lose focus on our true purpose and original objective.

I wrote a poem back in 2001 titled Lost that I believe also reflects this concept quite nicely.

Lost

Like a cork on the ocean
A leaf in the wildest storm
So my life has drifted
From the moment I was born
I stop sometimes and peer around
From the long grass that surrounds me
To get some idea of where I am
And where I am going
But it is only ever long enough
For me to realise that I am totally lost

Rod A Macpherson 2001

It is so easy to get caught up in the game of life and forget just how precious it really is just to be alive. We experience stress from endless emails, getting kids off to school, trying to manage a mortgage, relationships and of course our health. Throw into the mix the constant barrage of fear based material channelled through media on our televisions, and in our news, and the ineptitude of our political systems, it is understandable why we prefer to get lost and keep our heads below the long grass. It is challenging enough down here in our own swamp without looking even further beyond! We get to the stage where we start to believe that we really don't have time to follow our true purpose or even have a purpose for that matter! How sad is that, yet how true does that resonate?

In our personal lives, and in our businesses, we must never lose sight of our purpose. And remember that our purpose is something unique to us. It is ours alone and at the same time shared by all. If our purpose is our reason for being, and we are not following it with all of our heart and with all of our passion, then what is the point of our being? If we do not have a clear purpose we will feel lost. That could explain both business failure and suicide. We need to be consciously living our purpose for being.

And how exactly can we start living consciously? Firstly, by accepting the universal truth that we are all connected, and accepting that all of our thoughts and actions will have an impact somewhere else. We must take personal responsibility for our own lives and we must exercise choice in what we think, buy, vote for, in what we believe and in what we do and say. This does not require an enormous sacrifice. We are essentially fulfilling a worthy purpose by living consciously anyway. The important thing to remember is that it is up to each and every one of us, and not one or two of us, or politicians or school teachers. It is certainly not going to come from the media or corporate power brokers. It is up to us and it always was. I firmly believe that to be true.

When I say living consciously I mean taking the time to reflect before taking action. Still the mind and really feel into your choices and consider your responsibility as a healthy earth cell. Read the labels on your food and exercise choice to avoid chemicals and consume natural ingredients. Avoid preservatives. Invest a little more in organic produce. That means less poisonous chemicals going into our bodies and environment, and also more demand for wholesome naturally sourced food. Look to buy local product. This not only supports your own community but also reduces the damage from transport pollution. Think in terms of 'true cost'. The real cost of what you are buying. As I described in the previous chapter, this is the total cost to the environment in producing the product, and the cost to recycle it when it is obsolete, in addition to the true cost to the planet while you are using it.

Recycle what you can when you can. Look at the rubbish and waste that is not able to be recycled and ask yourself, can you reduce this waste by modifying your buying habits? Can you be more conscious in your product selection? Ask your product suppliers if they can influence their product wholesalers to reduce non-recyclable waste. The intention behind just one single phone to a manufacturer's feedback line can make such a positive difference. Be the one hundredth monkey.

Be selective in what you watch, and certainly what you accept as truth, on TV and read in news reports, remembering those that benefit most from our fear have control of the media. If we hear enough bad news we feel powerless and get into the 'well what can I do anyway?' mode. The principal role of mainstream media has become to keep us in fear and confusion. Confused and frightened consumers are so much easier to exploit. Remember always that we are in effect "powerful beyond measure". Do some of your own research on topics. Do not exclude any possibilities just because a supposed expert on your TV or radio said so. The very people who own or influence the media get to select that expert in the first place, and in any case **you can still see them**. They are just like you, still learning. They cast a reflection and are only expressing what they believe based on their own experiences, fears and prejudices.

The media decide whose opinion is aired. An example of this imbalance is in the climate change debate. More than ninety eight per cent of global scientists now agree that humans are impacting our climate yet the media will still hold a debate on that subject between two individual 'experts' with opposing views. That is not balanced news. The two per cent is getting the same coverage as the ninety eight per cent. This happens a lot with minority groups. In any case, the debate should be about what we are doing about climate change, but then that would have implications for the coal and oil industries that either own, or financially support, mainstream media. Are you getting the picture? Nothing is as it seems.

An old mate of mine, who is an accomplished conspiracy theorist, alerted me to the misuse of 'Global Warming' and

'Climate Change' as a smokescreen for the masses. I was initially dubious but, upon further explanation, it resonated with me. This ex school buddy has previously lived in a tree house out the back of Nimbin, in the hinterland of northern New South Wales, and is the master of the Facebook rant but he is no fool. The use of climate change as a central issue can be misleading. Remember that the ego controlled corporate gurus that sell us fear will do anything to hold on to their power. They are terrified of losing power because they do not yet know that they are powerful without their ego, and that their own light and love is so much more powerful than any money they could ever accumulate. We should feel sorry for them. By focussing our attention on climate change, through controlled media, they are able to direct the discussion to carbon solutions and lead us away from the real issue that is "Global Damage". As the debate rages over what the climate was a million years ago, or last century, we are ignoring the real harm to our waterways and land from damaging practices such as chemical spraying, genetic modification, over population, and of course polluting our oceans and rivers with plastic junk and chemicals. The debate should cover the whole spectrum not just a headline created to distract our attention. Be careful of that. Keep asking questions.

Questions are a powerful way of focussing attention and thereby raising awareness and consciousness.

Be more vocal with your views and ask more questions of your politicians and the businesses that you deal with. I currently shop at one of the supermarket giants, Woolworths (as well as local markets) and noticed that they had removed facial tissues made from recycled paper from their shelves.

I decided to move my business to Coles only to find that they had done the same thing. I asked both companies why these items had been removed and they stated that head office had taken them off the shelves due to low demand. Really? With the state of our environment there is not a demand for recycled paper tissues over those that require the destruction of our forests to manufacture? I don't think so. So I took the time to raise a complaint and received a delightfully worded response about how miserable they were not to be able to continue to stock the item due to low demand. This was obviously intended to garner some sympathy and to make me feel better. They even followed up with a survey to gauge how my complaint was handled and was I satisfied. Well I was not satisfied. I fired back along the lines "as a huge player, with unfair market dominance, it was up to them to stand up and take some responsibility and stock items that helped our environment, and that there were plenty of consumers that felt the same as me". I am not going to roll over on this. Most of us want to clean up our environment and using recycled product is a fantastic way to support that effort.

This is not about demand this is about consumers not getting their message heard. We have a responsibility to be heard. I do not personally like to think that I am blowing my nose into paper tissues made from trees specifically destroyed for that purpose. One would almost expect that established corporate citizens, such as Woolworths or Coles, would take responsibility and ensure that the environment was at the forefront of their product selection, or am I being naïve? They have immense power over their suppliers, just as we have immense power as consumers. These companies have feedback lines and, as customer focussed businesses, they will respond if the feedback is loud enough and often enough. We have the power. Make a call or, better still, demand the most sustainable products in person.

A recent example of the power of consciousness over greed is demonstrated in the failure of the proposed paper pulp mill development in my home state of Tasmania. The proposed site was on the picturesque Tamar River, a short drive north of Launceston. The site proposed by developers (Gunns Timber) was in the heart of a beautiful wine growing region and popular tourist route. My parents still have a delightful small acreage just across the river from the site. The proposal was to construct and operate a mill for the purpose of processing local Tasmanian forest to make pulp for paper production. Now lets examine that a bit more closely. Paper is a growth industry right? We are all reading more newspapers right? Bookstores and newsagencies are opening up everywhere right? To tear down perfectly good Tasmanian forest to make pulp with questionable environmental processes, on the beautiful Tamar River, was a good idea right? But wait, it would create more jobs so it must be good for us? Well conscious action, by those that saw through the charade as nothing more than exploitation of our natural resources for profit, was able to stop that project and eventually send the developers into liquidation. The financiers pulled out. This was an industry in the late stages of the cycle of life and death, nothing more, nothing less. Perhaps another option was to build a used timber recycling business or a tree seedling plant? I guess the return on investment did not stack up. This is a further example of the human obsession with money at the expense of life, and the futility of resisting natural cycles.

I have often said to my dear old dad, who still harbours a little bit of redneck Tasmanian in him, but who I also love and respect immensely, that there are unlimited jobs available for an unlimited time to anyone wanting work on the purpose of repairing our earth. We just need responsible and conscious government and business to fund it. And whom may I ask funds government and business? You guessed it, you and I. They rely on our support to exist.

If we say and do nothing then nothing changes. Have the courage to ask why?

Why is it that, despite this planet having access to an abundance of natural energy from the sun, we still mine coal and drill oil we know is poisoning our earthly body and slowly killing every one of us with it? Why is it that governments continue to poison water with fluoride, in the guise of oral health, when the evidence does not support its supposed benefits and when a healthy eating diet has always been the answer? How else would industry dispose of that junk? Pure clean water, as nature intended it, sustains all life on earth. Why would anyone even consider adding artificial chemicals to perfectly good life sustaining water?

Why do we allow misleading labelling on our food to continue? How hard is it to legislate that labelling must be clear, accurate and readable? Why do we continue to import toxic plastic bags to carry our groceries? What would it take to get rid of plastic completely? Why do we allow our oceans and rivers to be polluted when we know that clean water is the most valuable resource on the planet? Why do we allow ongoing development of our land, to house our burgeoning population, when we know that our planet is already hurting and cannot support it? Why do we continue to allow mineral exploration when we know that this industry is exploiting finite resources to feed unsustainable growth? Why do we ingest numerous drugs and potions, sold by grossly wealthy medical conglomerates, when we know that more people die from taking legally prescribed drugs than anything else and that wellness is simply a state of mind? And why do we spend billions of dollars on cures for cancer when we know that cancer is a symptom of the way we disrespect our environment and that the true cause of cancer is our own poisoning of our earth through greedy and fearful thoughts?

Because we are not living consciously, that is why. We must seek answers to these questions.

I said at the very beginning that I had plenty of questions. More than ever, I am really starting to appreciate the importance of asking these questions? Answers only come when the right questions are asked. It is simply not good enough for us to blindly accept what others, with blatantly obvious motives, tell us. Would you believe a thief that told you he would hold your wallet while you went swimming? Then why would you believe those that derive immense financial benefit from the extraction of coal seam gas when they say it is completely safe and that we need to keep mining the stuff? We all need to be asking a lot of questions before we take action or accept information as truth. Be brave and respect the power of your own light. The intention behind your questions directs focus and purpose that transforms your own light into a powerful laser.

If you have any doubt as to the power of the smaller parts of our universe look no further than the destruction an atomic explosion can cause. This is the energy produced from the splitting of a single atom! How many atoms in your body? You have immense power if you channel it with your intention. Before you go exploding all over the place, take a deep breath and remember who you really are in truth, and marvel at the power of your own intention.

Did you know that seven of the top ten biggest polluters in Australia are electricity providers? They are all named on Google. Despite this fact, our own government quibbled over a renewable energy target because these toxic emitters thought the target unfair! Seriously? Why do you think that is? Ask that question to yourself. Why would our biggest polluters and emitters of greenhouse gases be arguing that the target to reduce poisonous substances going into our system is unfair? Surely not money?

There are now a number of energy retailers offering alternatives to the big polluting energy companies. This gives you the choice of sourcing all of your energy from sustainable sources. Guess what will happen if these providers are hit with demand that outstrips supply? Producers will be encouraged to invest in more renewable energy generation to meet that demand. What would happen to coal fired energy polluters if demand for their product continues to drop, as it already is? They will go broke unless they change to meet the clean energy demand by consumers. We have the power and a responsibility to exercise it. The coal fired power industry is well into the death cycle and we should all let it rest in peace, as soon as possible.

Just as we require air to breathe to survive, so to do our largest polluters require capital. The sources of capital often come indirectly from us through either our combined deposits in banks or our superannuation savings. This is our money! We have a right, and dare I say, an obligation to ask that our money be invested in ethical institutions that enhance our wellbeing, not destroy it! Ethical investment funds only support ethical and environmentally sustainable businesses. If you have investments why not use one? A large private investment fund recently divested over $US1 billion from companies with exposure to coal due to the high financial risk. The coal business is not only a high financial risk it is a health risk!

I do not expect that everyone will have the motivation to do all of these things, but just by thinking differently, you will make a difference. Of course taking action is a more powerful use of intent, but pure and conscious thought matters. A conscious thought carries so much more power than the random subconscious thoughts that we generate every minute of our lives. A conscious thought is a focussed thought and more like a laser light compared to an ordinary torch beam. Every mindful thought and action makes a difference and strengthens that laser of consciousness.

I am reminded of that famous quote from the Chinese philosopher Lao-Tzu that "a journey of a thousand miles begins with a single step". Every little step counts and in fact is the only way forward. If we do not take that first step we go nowhere and nothing changes. Those gradual steps will eventually turn into a purposeful march!

Remember my diagram on conscious creation at the end of chapter seven? To create we must be able to feel what it is we want, reaffirm it and give gratitude for having it already. I have my own personal meditation, or mantra, that I use when wanting to reinforce my own personal power. It goes like this:

Thank you for this beautiful universe and the powerful love energy that flows through everything and flows through every particle of my being, connecting me to everything that is, making me a part of everything that is.

And, as a connected part of everything that is, I have access to all of the information that is known. All I have to do is ask and the answer will be given.

And, as a connected part of everything that is, I have access to unlimited healing energy. Healing love energy flows through me at all times. All I have to do is allow it.

And, as a connected part of everything that is, I am connected to all of the wealth and abundance that exists. I am separated from nothing. I have whatever I desire when I desire.

And, as a connected part of everything that is, I accept responsibility for that part of me that is not in alignment with love and compassion and I send that part of me love and forgiveness and ask that it return to love and peace.

I am truly blessed. Thank you.

The last part of my meditation acknowledges that we must also take personal responsibility for those parts of us that are stuck in fear and greed. We are not separate from that part. That is a part of us that we must accept exists and send it healing energy and loving thoughts. Do not fear it. As I alluded earlier, it is important to accept the 'what is' before you can consciously choose to change it.

Never underestimate the power of your own intentional thought when making a conscious decision to ask a question, or take a positive action, because it feels right to you, and you know in your own heart it is the right thing to do. You will feel great in the knowing that you are contributing to something so much bigger. This is the source of the power that will drive change.

Each and every single, focussed, intentional, conscious thought will combine like a laser light to create change. This is what Ghandi was referring to when he said "be the change that you wish to see in the world".

We simply have to learn to cooperate like healthy cells. We alone have that choice. We either make a decision to contribute consciously to a healthy existence on earth, just as we would expect from any healthy cell in our own bodies, or we continue to poison our host with our fearful thoughts and behaviours. We have that choice before us in every moment.

The solution lies in our thinking. Our thoughts create our perception of our world, which then becomes our reality. The ego is a thought machine. Without thought we have no fear. It is the ego that feels separation when in truth we are all connected. Remember who you really are. You are a spiritual being having a human experience. You are eternal. You make a difference. You are the difference.

We are all here for the human experience and I personally love it. I love my life on this earth. I feel honoured for being able to share our planet. I love talking with friends, following sport, running, walking, swimming and standing in the rain (this is starting to sound a bit like an dating site profile). But seriously, even though I accept that death is just a transition, I am not ready to let go of my human experience just yet. It matters to me. I believe that I contribute to a healthy planet. I also know that I am not perfect and that I can do better.

If you want a different human experience to the one that is manifesting around you then 'see' it differently. Challenge old thoughts and beliefs. Are your beliefs still relevant? As soon as you believe something it becomes true for you. As soon as you believe that you make a positive difference you will. Once you truly believe that you make a difference your actions will truly make a difference. They simply have to. It is simple science. Our actions are a direct result of our beliefs and thoughts and our thoughts influence the energetic field of life.

Let me take you back to my original theory on life.

All humans manifest as life on planet Earth in human form for the purpose of experiencing and learning together through those experiences. The purpose of life is to experience and learn and grow consciousness.

We are none of us perfect. It is ok to be imperfect. That is part of being human. I am asking that we all be a little more conscious and support and respect our earth. The Dalai Lama is no fool, although he still has a reflection so he is not perfect, yet his level of consciousness is high. He gets it. The experts that are chosen to grace our airwaves do not have all of the answers! Remember that everyone is always right, even when they are wrong. Do your own research and above all keep an open mind. Be prepared to listen and learn. Hold your beliefs lightly.

Be careful not to let your subconscious beliefs control you. Outside of a few universal truths, the rest of what we consider to be truth, is totally dependent on our own beliefs, and not truth at all. People everywhere foolishly defend their beliefs despite how they adversely impact, not only their own lives, but also all of our lives, and despite emerging evidence that continually challenges their validity. What would we fight for if we had no beliefs? What would we argue about? No one would be wrong or right. It is difficult to learn if we hold on to old ideas. It is ok to let old beliefs go. It is ok to admit they are obsolete and no longer serve us. It is certainly ok to change. Just ask this question of yourself. Are my beliefs serving both my greater self and me personally?

We feel when something is not right. We know. Truly 'see' yourself and others for who they really are beyond the perception of the mind. We learn little from talking. We learn more by observing and feeling. Challenge your beliefs. Be different. Honour your 'light' and exercise your choice. You cannot 'un-know' something. Ignoring your own power to create change is not a valid option.

Our choice is to be a healthy cell or a cancerous one, to be a part of the solution or a part of the problem. Every little thing matters and makes a difference. We may never understand why things happen. Why loved ones die too soon, why relationships end or the reason for catastrophic events. I know what I feel and I know there exists a much higher intelligence, and loving energy force, that maintains all life. Life has a purpose. What may seem like chaos is in fact in perfect order.

I am positive that everything that happens has a purpose. It is up to us to discover what that purpose is and pursue it with every fragment of our passion.

Namaste

Synopsis

We are all looking for real heroes. We want things to change but we don't know quite how to change things. We doubt our own power to make change.

There is no super hero coming to save us. Humanity is on the brink of extinction. The time is right here and now. Not tomorrow, now.

We experience life as a summary of our beliefs, but that is not who we are. We are certainly not what we do. We are unconditional love, manifesting as particles of indestructible, minute, spinning energy that is connected to everything that exists on earth, and is part of a greater universe in which nothing happens in isolation.

We are a part of a greater organism. We are not separate, even though we feel separation resulting from subconscious thoughts, filtered through a flawed belief system. We can choose our thoughts and therefore we can choose our beliefs. We have choice.

The mind is a powerful and potentially dangerous machine. Left unattended, it can do immense damage. Our life is simply our perception of what we think it is. Living in the present moment, beyond our beliefs and our mind, puts us in control of our lives. We create our life circumstances with thought.

Human beings are simply a part of all life. All living things live and die together. There are no winners without losers. We either all win or we all lose, all live or all die. The spirit, however, is eternal.

Human beings hold a position of privilege on this earth. With that privilege comes responsibility. We are all personally responsible for everything that happens on this planet.

Consciousness comes from being in the present moment, responding to the stimuli around us and not reacting to the thoughts within us.

Beyond the perception of our mind, and the illusion of our beliefs, lies the truth of who we really are.

We are powerful beyond measure. All you have to do is believe.

Rod A. Macpherson.

Printed in Great Britain
by Amazon